Your MIND
at Work

To Jack, Rupert and Oliver, Lana and Susan

To exist is to change, to change is to mature.
To mature is to go on creating oneself endlessly.

Henri Bergson, French philosopher

**RICHARD ISRAEL, HELEN WHITTEN
AND CLIFF SHAFFRAN**

Your MIND
at Work

Developing **Self-Knowledge**
for Business Success

**KOGAN
PAGE**

First published in 2000

Kogan Page Limited
120 Pentonville Road
London N1 9JN

British Library Cataloguing in Publication Data

A CIP record for this book is available from the British Library.

ISBN 0 7494 3059 1

Typeset by Saxon Graphics Ltd, Derby
Printed and bound in Great Britain by Clays Ltd, St Ives plc

Contents

About the Authors

RICHARD ISRAEL

Richard Israel is the author and co-author of numerous books, including *Sales Genius, BrainSmart Leader, Supersellf, The Vision* and *Brain Sell,* which has been translated into twelve languages. His work has been acclaimed by international media, including *Business Week, Success Magazine, Training & Development, The Miami Herald* and *The New York Sunday Times.*

Richard has integrated leading-edge brain research with his sales and marketing experience to create a sales model that consistently achieves outstanding results. He is a popular speaker at business and training conferences around the world and has appeared on numerous television and radio shows.

Richard is the originator of Inner Modeling®, a learning process used in the changing of behaviour and covert belief systems. More than one and a half million people across four continents have been trained with his materials. Today he is the President of Inner Modeling Inc, Vice-President of Dottino Consulting Group Inc, a partner in The Quicksilver Group, and an adjunct professor at Florida Atlantic University.

HELEN WHITTEN

Helen Whitten specializes in executive development and coaching and works with people in major organizations throughout the world. She has created a unique package of integrated solutions to address current personal and business challenges. Her methods enhance creativity, motivation and excellence in personal and team performance by enabling the development of an enthusiastic and optimistic attitude, clear goals consistent with personal values, practical skills and knowledge and the ability to maintain peak performance under pressure. The result is the development of integrated business practices that benefit the individual, the organization and society as a whole.

Helen is founder and Chief Executive of Positiveworks, London, a member of The Quicksilver Group. She has a post-graduate diploma in Personnel Management, and qualifications in cognitive-behavioural methodology, stress management and NLP. She is also a writer and broadcaster.

CLIFF SHAFFRAN

Cliff Shaffran is founder and Chairman of The Quicksilver Group, a unique consulting organization focusing on the human side of business. Its activities over the past 10 years with global clients have been devoted to how new knowledge is mediated into 'knowledge-in-use'.

Cliff has integrated ground-breaking research on the human brain with innovative workplace practices to produce a *thinking learning communicating*™ toolkit. Cliff's driving passion is developing individual human potential as the catalyst for team and organizational growth. He is a well-known and respected speaker, facilitator and business columnist.

Acknowledgements

The authors gratefully acknowledge the help of Raymond Walley of Success Dynamics, Croyden, for his input on the DiSC Personality Profile; Richard Cooke for his input on 'My Life' MindManager model; Stephen Palmer of the Centre for Stress Management, Blackheath, London SE3 7DH, for his input, training and support; Michael Jetter for his marvellous software program; Mike Morgan for his input on the Herrmann Brain Dominance Instrument; Chris Durkin, Pauline Wong and Sven Huebner of The Quicksilver Group for the graphics used in this book; and Rupert and Oliver Whitten for technical and moral support.

Preface

SETTING THE SCENE

In a recent workshop I was running in Hong Kong, one US executive reacted strongly to my suggestion that all participants map out as much about themselves as possible in five minutes. He sat defiantly, arms crossed, and said: 'I never think about myself, I don't like thinking about myself and I certainly don't aim to start now.'

Contrast this with a team of leading management consultants in Stockholm, who selected 'self' as one of their key relationships (after clients and staff). They knew, from years of practical experience, just how much self-knowledge counts. And in today's knowledge economy, where people are the only resource, self-knowledge is actually the key to both personal and organizational transformation.

My experience in Stockholm highlights two irrefutable reasons why there has never been a better time to read this book than now. The first reason is that knowing yourself is the key to building your own personal identity, creating an ever-increasing demand for you, as a brand. To do this, you need to be aware of your beliefs, values, feelings and vision, your levels of self-acceptance, self-confidence and self-expression, and your appreciation and understanding of your unique contribution.

The second reason is a new realization being shared by businesses across the world. It began in the United States around 1995, jumped the Atlantic to Europe and recently touched down in Asia. After all the downsizing, rightsizing and re-engineering, shareholders and corporate leaders are demanding more-with-less. And, not by coincidence, the deep well they can draw from is the massively untapped potential of their own people. They have discovered that the answers lie within, not without.

Developing organizations is all about raising individual and team capabilities to think, to learn and to communicate. And the basic ingredient is self-knowledge. So, from whichever direction you approach it, knowing yourself better will play a major part in shaping your career from now on.

We've asked many corporate leaders what it is that keeps them awake at night. Their answers are summed up in the business platforms shown in Figure 0.1. Working with the areas of communication, culture, change, innovation and performance is very different conceptually from focusing on the functional, such as production, distribution, marketing, administration and finance.

Sadly, the current training industry is way behind in its desperate attempts to develop the much needed team performance. Training basically focuses on technical skills and processes for the functional areas. This left-brain leftover from our traditional education system totally ignores the

Building Businesses in the Knowledge Economy
Growing financial and intellectual capital

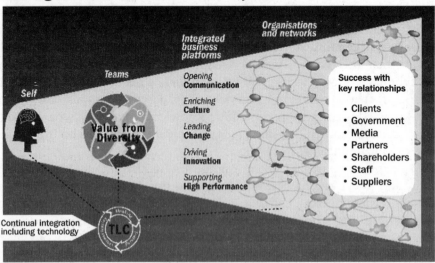

Figure 0.1 *Inside-out organizational transformation*

remarkable whole-brain potential that exists in every one of us. Unleash that personal potential and team performance improves exponentially. If you want real learning to take place, there must be both intellectual and emotional stimulation, otherwise the only thing achieved is mindless repetition.

So what does this mean to you and what can you do about it? To answer this question we must look at another powerful business trend. Leading business practice today is project- and network-based. People come together from all levels and functions, work fast and flexibly in teams, complete their projects, share their learning, disband and move to other teams. Some even work in a number of teams at once. In spite of this, millions are spent annually on team building, with the focus being *only* on the team. What participants learn about *themselves* is purely a secondary outcome.

Fortunately, this situation is also changing, as the very latest brain research is now being applied to business. The focus now is on developing self-knowledge simultaneously with building multi-disciplinary, cross-cultural, cross-functional teams. The simple reason for this is that the better you know yourself, the better you can understand and communicate with others. The basis of communication is trust, and that is what teams are all about.

No matter if you are 26 or 60, you now need to *unlearn* much of *how* you learnt at school and university and *relearn* how to read and record information, how to think and memorize, how to access your feelings and how to integrate it all with today's technology. The good news is that it can be done so much faster and more enjoyably with the whole-brain methodology outlined in this book.

It all boils down to knowing more, much more, about yourself. As you do, you will think more creatively, learn faster and become a better communicator: all vital prerequisites for raising your personal value in the high-performance teams that are going to drive organizations of the future.

This book is a comprehensive 21st-century toolkit. It is designed to get you started on the path to deeper self-knowledge. It will raise your thinking power by giving you an understanding of how your brain works, make you more aware of your emotional intelligence and leave you with a new outlook for marketing yourself, by seeing yourself as a brand.

This brings us to the very essence of your future business success. For career advancement in the knowledge society, which, as you will see, is project- and network-based, you need to place yourself where your strengths are most valuable and where you make the greatest contribution to each project outcome. There is no longer a simple line of promotion that takes you from clerk to CEO via production, marketing or finance.

No matter what your speciality, you also need to be a generalist. A generalist in thinking creatively, in understanding human behaviour, in synthesizing and mediating knowledge, and above all in communicating. Only when this is achieved can you expect your good ideas to be actually implemented.

Regarding yourself as a brand is an interesting concept. Brands are essentially the sum of all knowledge, experience and feelings for a product. The strength of any brand reflects the values behind it. Exactly the same applies to you. The better you know yourself, the better you can package yourself. And the better you can position yourself where you will be of greatest value.

Being of value in the resolution of complex issues is a good career driver (for example, 'let's get Joan in, she thinks well and will listen'). Complex situations do not resolve themselves: they are resolved by people, and, after five years of working with the thinking tools in this book, I am still amazed at how seemingly impossible situations are overcome by having team members look more closely at themselves.

Questions as simple as 'What helps or hinders you in the workplace?' or 'What ten things do you value most at work and at home?' have participants digging into the very depths of their being. Focusing on and comparing personal thoughts such as these often open participants to develop highly creative business solutions.

Too often people do not share their real feelings within a group. They bite their tongue rather than say when someone annoys them or when they disagree with their boss or colleagues. People need to express themselves honestly in a positive environment of open communication and trust. Teams are not built on destructive, personal criticism but on constructive, objective feedback. So, rather than people taking things personally, they focus on achieving common objectives. This positive environment produces the commitment that leads to high-performance results.

At the core of honest expression is self-knowledge. Everyone is totally unique: you are what your parents handed you, plus your life experiences. But how well do you know your own thinking and learning preferences, your own values and behaviour patterns? And, as a result, how well can you maximize the unique contribution you have to make in all situations?

Today you have a personal responsibility to know and to act. Your future depends on it.

Cliff Shaffran

1

Why Read This Book?

This book is written for those of you in the workplace who can see the benefit of understanding yourself better. Your ability to manage your career within the constantly changing business environment is directly determined by your ability to manage yourself. Self-knowledge is your guide to developing the confidence you require to meet whatever new challenges come your way. And there are plenty of challenges out there!

Have you ever considered yourself as a brand? To be able to sell your services as a continuing resource within your present job, or to gain a new position, you need to consider yourself as a 'brand' – just like Coca Cola or Ben and Jerry's ice cream. In order to do this, you need to examine yourself in relationship to your talents, preferences and opportunities. You need to be prepared to promote yourself as a needed resource, as the advertising companies might promote a product. It means asking yourself: 'What do I stand for? What can I offer? What is my unique contribution?' Without self-knowledge you may not be sufficiently aware of your strengths to 'package yourself up' in an attractive enough format to be able to do so.

This 'brand thyself approach' has arisen as a result of competition in a world that has opened up in an unprecedented way. The advances in technology during the 20th century have changed the face of work beyond recognition. Air travel and telecommunications have opened up markets that were previously inaccessible. You can talk to someone on the other side of the world as clearly as if they were in the nextdoor room. The internet has made the world accessible to anyone with a computer.

This global marketplace results in people in cold climates having access to exotic tropical fruits in their supermarket all year round. It means that you can do business 'virtually' through the World Wide Web on a 24-hour basis, with clients or suppliers you have never met, and with immediate results. An e-mail sent from Hong Kong reaches someone in the United States seconds later. A stock market change in New York affects the economy of the rest of the world within seconds.

This pace of change has transformed the very nature of business. It places new demands and pressures on all of us. Few people's lives are unaffected. Whether you are a fisherman on the beaches of India, a manager of a retail store in Dublin, or the chief executive of a multinational organization in Sydney, working lives have changed and businesses are under pressure from an increasingly competitive global economy.

Individuals must change their working practices to keep apace. You are likely to change career four or five times in a lifetime. Today's economic pressures on businesses may result in 'downsizing' and you may face redundancy at some stage in your career, for which you need to be prepared.

You need to be confident of your own ability to learn and adapt in order to manage your career in this new economy. Indeed, instead of perceiving change as a rug being pulled from under you, you must learn to dance on the ever-shifting carpet.

THE BENEFITS OF SELF-KNOWLEDGE

The age-old saying of 'Know thyself' is more true today than it has ever been if you are to successfully manage these challenges. When you know yourself better you maximize your strengths, overcome your weaknesses, improve your relationships, manage stress and greatly enhance your performance.

Figure 1.1 demonstrates the changes that have occurred in organizational life and in the lines of control and communication in recent years. When the structure of the modern-day organization was developed, at the time of the Industrial Revolution, it was common for a small number of owners or managers at the top of the hierarchy to make decisions for the whole company, without recourse to anyone else within the business. However, since that time, organizations have tended to flatten and open out and many are now working in a global network environment where

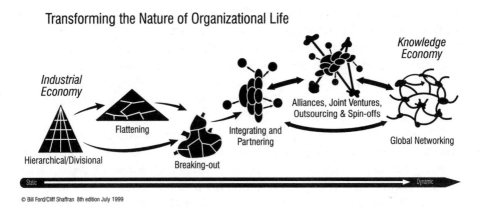

Figure 1.1 *From the hierarchical company to the global network*

anyone with a computer has immediate access and communication with the rest of the world.

In this global network, people in many different parts of a business are interfacing with clients and suppliers in the outside world and are having to make immediate decisions. At the top of an organization today, we can no longer expect to be able to 'tell' those below us what to do; if we are lower down in the organization we can no longer expect to be 'told' what to do. The ideal situation is for the top to listen to and take feedback from the bottom, and for the bottom to listen to and take feedback from the top. This top-down push, bottom-up push closes the gaps that exist between executives and the front line in so many organizations today.

Expectations and demands have changed along with the economic and technological circumstances. Now you need to be confident, knowledgeable, responsible and a decision-maker. You need to be able to learn new information fast and effectively and communicate with those around you, be they clients, colleagues or computers. Communication has become the most important factor of performance as you delegate without 'ordering', both supply and accept feedback, at the same time as interacting with people from diverse cultures.

Self-knowledge can help you manage these changes. Being aware of the effect that these situations are having on you allows you to make choices and to be in control. It can help you gain insights that improve both your quality of work performance as well as your quality of life by identifying how you think, how you learn and how you communicate most effectively. By understanding your own drives and motivations, you can question whether you are making the most of yourself and at the same time develop strategies to maximize your unique talents.

Self-knowledge is a continuous life-long journey of discovery. No one fully achieves it. However, when you can begin to see yourself as others see you, when you can appreciate your strengths, accept your vulnerabilities and continue to learn from your experiences, it is possible to develop a stronger sense of self. This sense of self acts as the navigator to help you manage the ups and downs and changes you will encounter during your working lifetime.

Self-knowledge is not something that is taught in any depth at school, university or even at business school. However, business leaders are coming to realize the benefits of this type of development within their organizations. Every bottom-line result has been achieved by a combination of human beings, whether they are programming a computer, operating a machine or making high-level strategic decisions. When you help each individual become aware of how they perform at their peak, you increase the capabilities of their team, their department and the whole organization. Knowledge and creativity now define a company's success: we are living in an era where brains have greater value than brawn. The more effective your thinking capacity, the more effective is your earning capacity.

There is more information on this subject today than at any previous time. Major developments have occurred in the understanding and application of research into the human brain and human behaviour in business in the last ten years, offering a whole new world of opportunities to improve human performance.

THE CONCEPT OF PACKAGING YOUR PERSONAL BRAND

This book is a practical guide to self-understanding and how to use that knowledge to design and build your own personal brand for business success. This in turn will improve your quality of life both in and out of the workplace.

How do you want people to see you? Can you identify internal competition? Do you know the unique benefits of your skills and talents? What differentiates you from other people? Do you enjoy high self-esteem? This book will help you answer these questions. It will help to develop your own 'brand personality' based upon awareness of your personal values, skills and behaviours.

Through this identification process you will learn how to develop your positive qualities and be in a stronger position to achieve your goals.

HOW TO USE THIS BOOK

The book is designed to hold up a mirror; to ask some questions that can help you develop intra-personal intelligence, or, in other words, the ability to maximize your potential through self-knowledge. We invite you to become involved and participate in the process. We suggest that you look at yourself and answer the questions asked in this book as honestly as you are able. This can take some courage, but there is much to be gained from taking an objective view.

To maximize your investment in this book, do all the exercises and quizzes. These exercises are designed to be completed speedily. We have suggested the times required for each. Work fast: you will discover that your brain can work fast enough to complete the exercises in the suggested time. Make notes, draw or doodle in the journal section at the back or in the margins. Let the book be your guide, asking you questions about yourself that you may not previously have considered.

Our learning methodology is based on a three-step process and each chapter contains the following ingredients:

1. identification and awareness of your present situation;
2. analysis of how you are managing yourself and your career; and
3. practical models and methodologies to set and achieve your goals.

MAPPING

Throughout this book exercises are shown as 'business maps' reproduced on 'The MindManager' software, © MindJET LLC, 1994–1999. You will encounter many of these maps throughout the book and they are adapted from a form of note-taking known as 'mind mapping', originated by Tony Buzan. You will see instructions on how to build the business maps next to the exercises concerned.

THE LAYOUT OF THE BOOK

We have divided the book into three parts, each building on the previous one, to allow you to build effective self-knowledge. In Part One, 'How You Got Here Today', you have the opportunity to investigate your performance to date: how have you reached where you are today, and what has driven and influenced you? Without awareness you cannot know what exists to be changed. This section is designed to shed light on the thoughts and actions that have brought you to this point.

Secondly, in Part Two, 'Who is Navigating?', by analysing your current business practices and performance you learn if your present behaviours are taking you where you want to go.

Thirdly, in Part Three, 'Looking at the Future', you can develop strategies to support your personal goals, through the insights gained in the first two parts.

In the following pages you will discover the TLC Toolkit. TLC stands for 'Thinking, Learning and Communicating', the 'tender loving care' alternative to keep you successful in today's workplace. The TLC Toolkit represents a set of practical techniques and methodologies, drawn from practical case studies and business experience. All this helps you to learn how to think, to think how to learn and, finally, to communicate it all successfully. The TLC Toolkit is an effective way to develop self-knowledge and enhance personal and team performance.

Enjoy the process of self-discovery. Be fascinated by your uniqueness, celebrate your successes and realize that this new knowledge is the key to your future success.

INTRODUCTORY SELF-AWARENESS QUESTIONNAIRES

The following seven questionnaires help you to reflect on your present state of self-awareness. All exercises are designed to be undertaken at speed, so take 2–5 minutes on each exercise.

EXERCISE 1.1 SELF-AWARENESS CHECK

On a scale of 0–10 mark down how self-aware you feel you are at the moment

0   1   2   3   4   5   6   7   8   9   10

What mark would you like to achieve by the end of the book?

EXERCISE 1.2 HOW WELL ARE YOU MANAGING WORKPLACE CHANGE?

Place a tick in the column which best answers the following questions.

	How often are you aware of:	Frequently	Sometimes	Rarely	Never
1.	Feeling overwhelmed by your daily commitments?				
2.	Feeling unable to keep up with the latest technology?				
3.	Feeling guilty that you are too tired to enjoy the time you have with:				
	your partner?				
	your children?				
	your family?				
	your friends?				
4.	Having to stay late at the office?				
5.	Feeling too tired to think straight?				
6.	Feeling too stressed to make a good decision?				
7.	Feeling angry at the demands made of you?				
8.	Feeling disillusioned at the lack of support from colleagues?				
9.	Feeling disillusioned at the lack of recognition from superiors?				
10.	Feeling you do not have adequate skills to manage your workload?				
11.	Feeling that you may be one of the next to be downsized?				
12.	Feeling you do not have transferable skills if your job situation were to change?				
13.	Feeling unable to balance your life between work and home?				

How often are you aware of:	Frequently	Sometimes	Rarely	Never
14. Feeling your performance is hampered by the number of distractions in your working environment?				
15. Feeling unable to motivate yourself?				
16. Feeling you have not got a clear idea of what you want from your working life?				
17. Lacking self-confidence to manage change?				
18. Feeling powerless to influence your present situation?				
19. Blaming others for your present situation?				
20. Not knowing what action to take for the best?				

Scoring: Score 4 for Frequently, 3 for Sometimes, 2 for Often and 1 for Never. Any mark over 60 denotes that you could benefit from concentrating on developing strategies to manage your stress levels. You will find information on this in Chapter 8. The next series of exercises, 3 to 6, are designed to elicit your present thinking on work.

EXERCISE 1.3 YOUR DEFINITION OF SUCCESS

Take two minutes to consider how you would define a successful person. Figure 1.2 is a template of a 'business map' to work from. The map revolves around the central topic in the middle and it is best for you to allow your thinking to develop as fast as possible with the associated words or short phrases relating to your definition of success. Write down anything that comes into your mind. You can have as many branches and ideas coming from the central image as you like. Write the words on the lines, or draw pictures to symbolize your ideas about a successful person.

Success can be defined in many different ways that are personal to you. For example, some people define success through family and relationships, others by material goods and money, others by quality of life or happiness, others would value expertise more than financial reward (for example, an

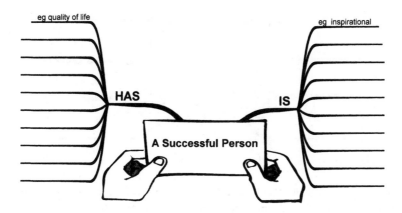

eg quality of life

eg inspirational

HAS

IS

A Successful Person

Figure 1.2 *A successful person*

academic or musician may not earn vast sums but could still be very 'successful'). Consider your own view of success on Figure 1.2.

1. How many of the above criteria have you personally already achieved?

_____

_____

_____

2. For how many of the above criteria have you defined strategies to achieve in the future?

_____

_____

_____

EXERCISE 1.4 WORK PURPOSE

Take two minutes now to consider your present motives for working (eg, 'The reason I work is to earn money'). Write them down on Figure 1.3.

Figure 1.3   *'The reason I work'*

1. When you look at your responses to this question, do you find that your present work is satisfying these reasons?

_____

_____

_____

2. If not, what changes might you make?

_____

_____

_____

EXERCISE 1.5 WORK ENVIRONMENT

Without focusing specifically on your present position, consider the ideal surroundings and people you enjoy working with. Write your answers down on Figure 1.4.

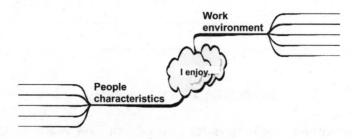

Figure 1.4   *MindManager Map on 'The kind of work environment I enjoy'*

Consider whether you can find these qualities in your present work colleagues. Could these qualities exist in them without your having noticed them before? Do you think your colleagues could describe you in this way?

Are there any changes you can make to your present work environment to create more of these aspects in your present post?

_____

_____

_____

_____

_____

_____

EXERCISE 1.6 CAREER VIEW

How clear a view do you have of your future career path? Draw a picture of a path across the page, below, to represent your career up to this point, then take the path forward to represent your future.

Look at the path you have drawn and consider how clear your view of the future is. Look at the shape of the path and see if it gives you any indications of your feelings about your career. Is the path winding or straight? Is it muddy or made of concrete? Does it go back on itself anywhere, or turn circles? Write any comments below.

_____

_____

_____

EXERCISE 1.7 THINKING QUIZ

How well do you understand your present thinking process? The following quiz will help to determine your answer. Answer True or False to the following 20 statements.

1.	The quality of your thinking has a direct effect on your life.	True	False
2.	All thinking starts with your belief systems, many of which are subconscious.	True	False
3.	Your behaviours influence other people's belief systems.	True	False
4.	In a position of authority the people that report to you model your behaviours.	True	False
5.	Every new situation you face triggers off an internal emotional response.	True	False
6.	Your thinking has little relationship to the quality of your life.	True	False
7.	Thinking affects your physical chemistry.	True	False
8.	Some successful business organizations are using sports psychologists to coach their teams in success.	True	False
9.	There is a human tendency to believe you are a lot smarter than you really are.	True	False
10.	Intelligence is something you are born with and cannot be developed.	True	False
11.	When a stressful message is received into the brain through the senses, a physical response takes place in the body.	True	False
12.	To a large extent you can control your own stress.	True	False
13.	Negative and/or irrational thinking has no effect on stress reactions.	True	False
14.	Studies of the human brain show that information that is not reinforced by review and/or follow-up within 24 hours has up to an 80 per cent evaporation rate.	True	False
15.	Successful people do not need to have written goals or missions.	True	False
16.	A repeated thought builds up a chemical pathway that develops a thinking and behavioural habit.	True	False
17.	The power of visualization is one of the most powerful ways of helping you to manage yourself.	True	False
18.	Meditation is a recognized method of reducing stress and burnout.	True	False
19.	Being assertive means respecting one's self and giving respect to others.	True	False
20.	Body language accounts for up to 58 per cent of a communicated face-to-face message.	True	False

Answers: Mark one point for each of the following:

True: numbers 1, 2, 3, 4, 5, 7, 8, 11, 12, 14, 16, 17, 18, 19, 20

False: numbers 6, 9, 10, 13, 15

If you scored 18 or more, you already have an excellent understanding of your thinking processes. This book will help you gain further expertise. If you scored less than 18, this book will assist you in learning how to develop successful thinking processes.

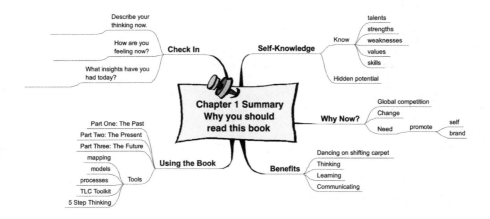

Figure 1.5   *Summary: why you should read this book*

PART ONE

HOW YOU GOT HERE TODAY

2

Beliefs Drive Actions

There are many factors to be considered on the journey to self-knowledge. This is not a 'soft' skill but is an important factor both in successful communication and in living a healthy, balanced life. Throughout this book you will study these issues in detail so you can better understand yourself, and learn how to be ever more successful.

This process of understanding and change is covered in the 'Five-Step Thinking System'.

FIVE-STEP THINKING SYSTEM

Step One: Beliefs and values	Your beliefs and value systems are generated from influences around you through your lifetime.
Step Two: Thoughts and expectations	These beliefs and values influence your thoughts and expectations of life and how you interact with yourself, others and the world at large.
Step Three: Emotions	Beliefs, values, thoughts and expectations drive your emotions. If you are thinking negative thoughts, for example, you may feel anxious; if you are thinking positive thoughts, you are likely to feel calmer.

Step Four: Behaviours	Your emotions and your thoughts directly affect your behaviour. If you feel nervous, you are likely to behave less assertively than if you feel confident.
Step Five: Actions	All of the previous steps influence the actions you choose to take in your life. In this context the term 'behaviour' means *how* you do something; the term 'action' means *what* you do.

Figure 2.1 is a graphical representation of the Five-Step Thinking System.

An example of this process might be a belief that 'a job is for life'. This might drive your thoughts and expectations to feel angry if your job was threatened. You might think: 'This should not be happening to me.' Your behaviour could become aggressive at the meeting where you hear about your possible job loss and you might take action by choosing to resign in order to gain a sense of control

IDENTIFYING BELIEFS

Your first step is to identify what beliefs have influenced you up to this point in time. Beliefs are ways of thinking and behaving that are literally

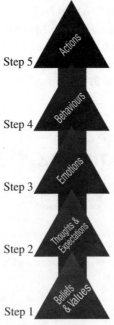

Figure 2.1 *The Five-Step Thinking System*

'soaked up' from our parents, teachers and role models from day one. They are your acceptance of a set of values and social and moral guidelines that shape everything you do.

This could be the religion your parents did or did not practise, or maybe the type of diet you were offered – 'carrots make you see in the dark' or 'it is cruel to eat meat'. Perhaps boys were treated with greater respect than girls, or vice versa. Or boys were not supposed to be emotional – 'boys don't cry'.

Did your parents tell you to 'get a job and keep it'? Or that to enter a profession meant you would have 'a job for life'?

You can hear people express beliefs at work when you hear such statements as 'that will never work here' or 'they will never accept that', although the speaker may not have tested the suggestion out in recent times. We therefore add to our beliefs continually. They shape our opinions and assumptions about situations and about people.

Have you adopted beliefs and values to gain approval? As human beings we seek approval from our elders and peers as this is both natural and is closely linked to survival. There is a strong need to bond and belong to families and to communities, and a business organization is no exception. Working within a system often guarantees an easier career path, so it takes maturity and self-confidence to challenge the customs and beliefs of those you work with.

However, having the courage to ask the simple question 'why?' can have extremely beneficial results. Take the air hostess at United Airlines who was serving coffee to passengers. She had to place a paper lid on the coffee jugs before she served, only to remove the lids and throw them away as she came to pour the coffee. Eventually she questioned the need for the lids. Her simple question saved the airline approximately US $60,000 per year. A belief that it was better to serve coffee from jugs with lids was no longer appropriate.

Beliefs are so pervasive a part of your make-up that it can be difficult to notice them as they become automatic responses. It can take years before you have truly identified and questioned your own set of beliefs.

Building beliefs is like learning to drive. When you first learnt to drive a car, you were aware of all the thoughts and actions you needed to take to pass the test. As driving becomes a habit, you no longer pay conscious attention to 'how to' drive, but only to your destination. The process of driving becomes automatic. In a similar way, the habits resulting from your belief systems affect the way you think, learn and communicate and yet you can be totally unaware of these silent forces at work.

The first thing to do is to question some of your conditioned responses to situations and identify whether they are appropriate to your life today.

EXERCISE 2.1 I BELIEVE

1. Write down your beliefs by focusing your attention on your work activities, your boss, your colleagues, your clients (eg, 'I believe I must have the approval of my colleagues').

    _____

    _____

    _____

    _____

    _____

    _____

    _____

    _____

2. Write down the responses copied from parents or teachers (eg, 'I believe you must work very hard to succeed' or 'I believe a leopard never changes its spots').

    _____

    _____

    _____

    _____

    _____

    _____

    _____

    _____

3. Write down any insights gained from this exercise.

_____

_____

_____

_____

_____

_____

_____

_____

_____

Your beliefs tend to shape your values. Your values are a measurement of the worth you place on the things around you. For example, you may place a higher value on your health than on your material possessions, or vice versa. In the next exercise you have an opportunity to identify and question your own values. You can then assess whether your values are forming your priorities as to how you spend your time.

EXERCISE 2.2 VALUE CLARIFICATION

1. In column 1 of the table overfleaf, 'what is important to me', rate your top ten values in order of importance, with 1 being the highest.

Now that you have established what you believe are your top ten values, this exercise will display the day-to-day reality of your value system.

2. In column 2, list the top ten values according to how you spend your time, in order of importance.

When reviewing the differences between column 1 and column 2, you will see a snapshot of what your values are and will gain insight into the beliefs that have driven those value sets. You might also discover a personal dilemma between what is important to you versus how you are spending your time.

	Column 1 (What is important to me)	Column 2 (How I spend my time)
Meaningful work		
Security		
Love		
Family		
Friendship		
Competition		
Status		
Personal growth		
Health		
Community service		
Adventure		
World peace		
Spirituality		
Making a difference		
Peace of mind		
Wealth		
Cooperation		
Power		
Happiness		
Integrity		
Recognition		
Patriotism		
Respect		
Loyalty		
Independence		
Wisdom		
Teamwork		
Leisure		
Variety		

3. Write down the changes you intend to make as a result of these insights.

_____

_____

_____

Did you notice any differences between values regarding your personal life and business life?

_____

_____

_____

EXERCISE 2.3 MOST IMPORTANT THINGS

The following exercise is reproduced on the MindManager mapping software, as are many of the exercises in this book. Use the branches to record your thoughts. Put a word or a short sentence on top of each line. Alternatively you can use a symbolic picture. Allow your mind to work freely and speedily to note anything you feel relevant.

Exercise 2.3 allows you to consider the most important areas of your life, both at home and at work. As a suggestion, list up to ten items for each section; these can include people, activities and/or things.

Acting on the values that are important develops a new you, and one that is not acting on automatic pilot. Perhaps you need to update earlier sets of beliefs and customs that you may have outgrown. Or you may need to reconfirm values, beliefs and customs that have been influencing you.

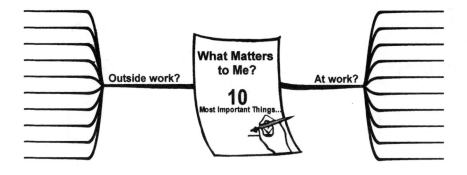

Figure 2.2   *MindManager Map on 'What matters to me?'*

EXERCISE 2.4 INFLUENCES AND ROLE MODELS

1. What are the main messages your parents, family, friends, and teachers told you about how you should handle your work life? Were you influenced by any fictional characters? Allow your mind to work fast, and record your thoughts.

I must. . . (eg, 'I must get things right')

_____

_____

_____

_____

I should. . . (eg, 'I should be able to pass all my exams')

_____

_____

_____

_____

Other people must. . . (eg, 'Other people must understand my problems')

_____

_____

_____

_____

Other people should. . . (eg, 'Other people should mind their own business')

_____

_____

_____

_____

_____

The world is. . . (eg, 'The world is full of strife')

_____

_____

_____

_____

_____

_____

Continue with any other thoughts you have on this.

_____

_____

_____

_____

_____

_____

_____

_____

_____

EXERCISE 2.5 PULLED OR SHOVED?

Think about your present job and consider whether you were pulled towards it by your own enthusiasm or shoved by parental, academic or economic influences.

1. Who influenced you to take your current position?

_____

_____

_____

_____

_____

2. If you were able to choose again, what choices would you make?

_____

_____

_____

_____

_____

_____

BELIEF SYSTEMS

It is time to review and update your belief systems. Perhaps through the passage of time some beliefs are not serving you as well as they have in the past. Or maybe you have belief systems that need reinforcing. The next exercise will assist you in this.

EXERCISE 2.6 REPEAT OR DELETE

Go back over Exercise 2.1 with a coloured highlighter and mark all the belief systems you would like to repeat or emphasize. Use a black pen to cross out all the belief systems you wish to delete and write in any new belief systems you wish to establish below.

_____

_____

_____

_____

_____

_____

Beliefs colour and shape your thoughts and result in behaviours which are key to your business success. You now have the techniques to become more *aware* of these influences as well as to re-evaluate if they both support and reflect the person you are today.

Defining values and beliefs results in higher self-esteem through a greater sense of self. It also improves decision-making as it acts as a navigator towards your goals.

We were working with a young manager recently who was asked to dismiss two employees without full legal benefits. Officially these people had done nothing wrong. The young manager was extremely uncomfortable about this as it went against his value system. Having thought about it for some time, he went to his senior manager and discussed the problem. He did not want to work in a position where he had to act contrary to his beliefs and so he allowed this to guide his decision. Fortunately he was able to negotiate a transfer to another post.

ROLE MODELLING IS A TWO-WAY PROCESS

You are influencing other people's belief systems. Whatever your position, others are watching you and copying you. The reason for this is that one way the human brain learns is by mimicking. Therefore, be conscious of how you think, behave and talk in public and monitor your own responses. Language is particularly important, and if you want a 'can do' environment then you need to ensure that the verbal cues you send people reflect 'can do' thinking in yourself first. See Figure 2.3.

EXERCISE 2.7 I AM A ROLE MODEL TO. . .

Exercise 2.4 prompted you to consider the people who have been your role models. Now consider to whom you may be a role model yourself.

1. Write down as many people you can think of to whom you may be a role model.

_____

_____

_____

_____

_____

_____

Figure 2.3 *Two-way role modelling*

2. Are you happy with the model you are projecting? If not, what changes would you like to make?

_____

_____

_____

_____

_____

_____

Continue to consider the influence you are having on those around you and use the following exercise to decide how you would like to be remembered when you retire. This gives you an opportunity to consider the balance you would like to maintain in your life now, in order to reflect the impressions you would like to leave.

EXERCISE 2.8 MY 85TH BIRTHDAY PARTY

Imagine you are holding your 85th birthday party. Three people will be making speeches about you. One is a family member, one is a friend and one is a former colleague. Write three or four sentences encapsulating what you would like them to say about you in their speech.

1. The family member:

_____

_____

_____

_____

_____

_____

2. The friend:

_____

_____

_____

_____

_____

3. The former colleague:

_____

_____

_____

_____

_____

_____

When you look at these sentences, you will become aware that what you have said highlights the personal qualities that you value in yourself. Consider what actions and behaviours you can focus on to ensure that you radiate these qualities more often to those around you.

_____

_____

_____

_____

_____

_____

Are you working from home? If so, finding role models, bonding and mimicking can be difficult. This can be a lonely situation and it is difficult to know what is happening at the organization or to learn what are the 'accepted behaviours' if you are not there.

If you are working from home, it is equally important to know your own personal beliefs and values so that they can guide you in your daily decisions. Make a point to check your value system with that of the team you are working with by sharing and identifying priorities. Most companies and many departments now have value statements with which employees can align themselves.

You are, consciously or unconsciously, building beliefs throughout your lifetime. They represent a set of filters through which you see yourself and the world; they shape your perspectives and prejudices and the decisions that you make. You develop them to help you gain a sense of control and to manage the many situations you face.

These perspectives may or may not be objective or rational. What was an appropriate viewpoint in early life may not be either helpful or suitable as an adult working in a multi-cultural workforce. Consider also the fact that

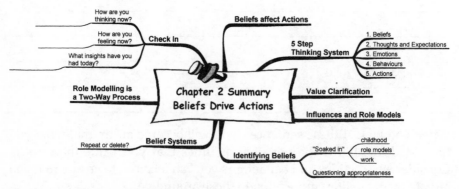

Figure 2.4   *Summary: beliefs drive actions*

you are now a 'brand' and are presenting yourself as such. Do your current beliefs align themselves to the brand you wish to portray? It is a good idea for you to repeat this chapter yearly, making it your 'values check-up'!

In the next chapter, you will discover how the influences and beliefs you have uncovered in this chapter are affecting your thinking patterns and expectations.

3

Thinking About Thinking

In the previous chapter, we investigated how the experiences and influences you have been exposed to affect your values and beliefs. In the fast-changing business world it is essential to keep questioning your perceptions, perspectives and attitudes. This challenges the thoughts that have shaped your mindset. It will also help you decide which thought patterns are still benefiting you today.

Human beings have the powerful capacity to think about their thinking and to reflect on their own attitudes – 'I think, therefore I am.' Every action, service or product starts with a human thought. For example, you are probably aware of an 'inner voice' in your head. The thoughts from your inner voice are physical realities that affect your performance, your body language and even your health. It is easy, however, to forget the important part they play in your life simply because you cannot see them.

Today scientists are revealing the way in which thoughts affect the chemical make-up of the body. Research by Dr F Happe of the Institute of Psychiatry in London shows that there is a specific area of your brain responsible for the type of reflective thinking you are doing while reading this book.

Research has shown that taking exercise similarly affects the chemical make-up of the brain. Indeed exercise is now a common part of any therapeutic process. The main response to this information has been predominantly in the field of physical fitness. Recent years have seen a complete new industry develop in the area of health and nutrition. Drive through any major city and you will see endless health clubs and health stores catering for all income groups. Notice how many people are jogging, roller-skating, cycling and queuing up for a tennis court. Bookstores offer dozens of publications on health and fitness, with every type of sports activity imaginable. Even fast food restaurants are now offering health-conscious options, and food packaging lists the nutritional composition and ingredients.

Forward-thinking organizations are installing gymnasiums within their buildings or arranging discounts at nearby health clubs. Such companies are aware that it is beneficial, in terms of both work performance, image and reduced health costs, to keep their employees fit and energetic, and that offering these facilities on-site saves employees' travelling time.

More organizations are now also helping employees to develop a healthy mind. The quality of thinking within a company affects creativity, morale, community and ultimately bottom-line results. As companies become interested in the quality of their staff's thinking, we see a new item appearing in their balance sheet: 'intellectual capital'.

THOUGHT FILTERS

To understand the importance of monitoring your thinking, it may help to imagine jumping into a swimming pool whose water has not been filtered but is filled with green algae and bacteria. Would that appeal to you? Or would you demand a higher standard of water to refresh your body?

Negative thinking is the equivalent of green algae in your mind. It is just as important, therefore, to filter the thoughts that enter your mind. To have crystal-clear thinking, you need to be conscious of the quality of the thoughts you let in. Whereas you might not be conscious about your belief systems, you can certainly become aware of your thoughts as they enter your mind.

It is estimated that you have approximately 40,000 thoughts every day, and that a majority are negative. Also you repeat between 55 and 65 per cent from the previous day. So a good deal of what you thought about yesterday you repeat day after day. Ask yourself: 'Is my thinking resulting in the quality of life I desire?'

Think of your brain working on a debit and credit accounting system, ie it carries forward a daily balance. So if you had 25,000 negative thoughts and 15,000 positive thoughts today, you would be carrying forward 10,000 negative thoughts for tomorrow.

All this has a compounding effect. You might have noticed how one little molehill can grow into a mountain over a period of time, resulting in your becoming stressed and aggravated seemingly for no real reason at all. For example, someone forgets to greet you at work. Immediately your mind begins to wonder what you did wrong. If you were to dwell on this for the next few hours you could end up believing that you are about to be fired, whereas the person ignoring you might have just have had something else on their mind. The resultant fear came only from your thinking.

EXERCISE 3.1 THE THOUGHT POOL

Take an intuitive guess as to how well your mental filter is working. If you had to swim in the pool of your thoughts, would that pool be clear or would it be murky? Write a few words to describe the general state of your thinking over the last two days.

_____

_____

_____

THE MENTAL FILTER

The way to develop an effective mental filter is to become increasingly aware of your thoughts on a minute-by-minute basis. This helps you understand how you are shaping both your business and your personal life.

Just as you have habitual ways of behaving – waking up at the same time, taking the same route to work, eating meals at a particular place or time – you also have habitual ways of thinking. The first step to switching on your own mental filter is to become *aware* of your thinking patterns and the beliefs or expectations that drive them. These habitual thinking patterns will have played a part in conditioning your responses and also in helping you to create the business life you are presently experiencing.

Thoughts, just like beliefs, can become automatic. When you have a thought for the first time, you are conscious of it. The more often you have that thought, the more likely it is to become a habit and develop into an unconscious thought pattern. Here are some exercises to help you to identify your thoughts, understand what you are thinking and how you came to develop them.

In the process of completing these exercises, you can identify whether your thinking is helping or hindering you. You will be able to monitor your positive/negative thinking, and examine how effective your present thinking strategies are.

EXERCISE 3.2 WHAT AM I THINKING?

How do you become *aware* of your present thinking, in the rush of everyday life? You need to set up a trigger to allow you to take a thought check. First, decide on your trigger – for example, every time you take out your wallet or purse, or every time you stop for a drink or meal. When this trigger occurs, you immediately note your thinking. Was it positive or negative, was it focused or was it stressed?

Positive	Negative
Eg, I can manage this situation.	Eg, I will never get this done in time.

By noting the results of all the scores for a day, you then have a sample of the balance of positive and negative thoughts. If your thinking is weighted towards positive, you are certainly working in the right direction. If your score is weighted towards doubts and negativity, you are receiving a warning sign that your thinking is detrimental to your business and social health.

You may like to write down some initial thoughts here. What are you presently thinking?

_____

_____

_____

_____

_____

_____

This random check can give you insights into the quality of your thoughts. You may well like to repeat this exercise every few months as a mental check-up.

THE CHEMISTRY OF THINKING

Thoughts become physical realities in our brains. Each human brain looks physically much like another. They weigh approximately 1.35 kg in men, or 1.25 kg in women. Your unique personality is the result of each thought and experience as it is recorded in your brain, through chemical interactions.

Each time you think, learn, imagine or remember, a brain cell fires a combination of chemicals to another brain cell. Both cells can send and receive messages. This activity forms a memory trace, or neural pathway, in your brain tissue. The chemicals involved in creating these neural pathways are known as neurotransmitters. Each brain cell has a receptor into which the neurotransmitters fit, like an electric plug and socket. Just as when you connect an electric plug to a socket the current flows, enabling you to switch on a light or appliance, so the connection in your brain sends a message flow through your body. This enables you to take your chosen action.

Watching live brain cells move is similar to watching two people holding out their hands to one another, seeking to make physical connection. The dendrites and axons, which are the finger-like tendrils on the brain cell through which the neurotransmitters pass, actively search for contact with other cells. The neural pathways are created as the message is fired from one cell to another across what is referred to as the 'synaptic gap' between cells. It is for this reason that you need to monitor your thoughts, as it is the development of these thought pathways that leads us to repeat thoughts. You can see the thought process in Figure 3.1.

From one conscious moment to the next, your brain is changing and developing according to your thoughts, emotions and behaviours. The nature of the chemical released varies according to the experience or message to which your brain is responding. Therefore the chemistry in your body changes depending on your thinking. This will be covered in more detail in Chapter 9, 'The Pressure Pot', in which we discuss how stress can affect your emotional and physical well-being.

Although each thought and action is recorded in your brain, you are only conscious of a small percentage of this activity. Some neural messages are

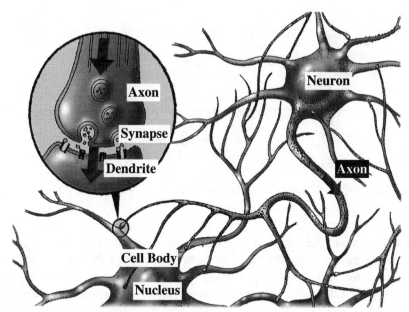

Image labels: Axon, Neuron, Synapse, Dendrite, Axon, Cell Body, Nucleus

Figure 3.1 *Active thought-process*

conscious thoughts; others are working on an unconscious or automatic level.

When you consider the millions of activities that are occurring within your body, all travelling through the brain, it is hardly surprising that it is necessary for these to be below your consciousness. As you drive a car, for example, your brain is calculating your speed, the curves of the road, the activities of the cars around you, making conversation with a passenger, watching the landscape, and listening to music on the cassette. At the same time, brain signals ensure that your heart beats, your lungs inflate, your digestive system processes your breakfast, and much more. If you were conscious of all these activities your mind would be overwhelmed. See Figure 3.2.

THINKING HABITS

'We are what we repeatedly do. Excellence, then, is not an act, but a habit.' *(Aristotle)*

Think back over your life to where certain thinking patterns dominated you: a loss of a sweetheart, a holiday or exams. For example, during your

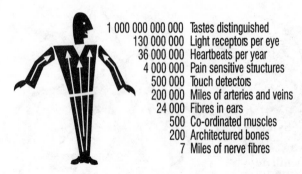

1 000 000 000 000 Tastes distinguished
130 000 000 Light receptors per eye
36 000 000 Heartbeats per year
4 000 000 Pain sensitive structures
500 000 Touch detectors
200 000 Miles of arteries and veins
24 000 Fibres in ears
500 Co-ordinated muscles
200 Architectured bones
7 Miles of nerve fibres

Figure 3.2   *The human mind and the human body*

final exams at school or university, when you were engrossed in certain subjects, all your thinking was centred upon passing the exam. Some of those subjects may now be a distant memory, as your thoughts and activities have switched to other priorities. This is the way that your memory works, filing away those thoughts that are not being used on a daily basis so that they are harder to access. What you focus your mind on is what becomes the information stored in your short-term memory and is easier to access. It is these predominant thinking patterns that you are investigating now in order to decide whether your present thoughts are supporting or sabotaging your work performance.

Thoughts become habits as the connection between cells strengthens. Each time you repeat a thought it is more likely to become a habit. This is why teachers use the rote-learning system, so that the information you need to remember for exams becomes a thought pattern in your brain.

Developing a thinking pathway is like walking through a wheatfield. The first time you enter the field you need to push your way through the wheat to create a path. Similarly in the brain, the chemicals have to push their way across the synaptic gap between cells. Like learning something new, or changing a habit, this can feel unfamiliar and uncomfortable at first. However, the more you walk through a wheatfield, the clearer the path becomes. The more often you have a thought, the more easily the message passes from one cell to another. See Figure 3.3.

This efficient system works well for constructive thinking and makes it easy for you to continuously learn and remember. Remember, though, it works against you in negative thinking. When you build strong connections of negative thoughts it becomes easier for you to keep repeating those negative thought patterns. See Figure 3.4.

It is important to identify any negative thoughts, or what can be called the inner critical voice, and to change them to something that is more

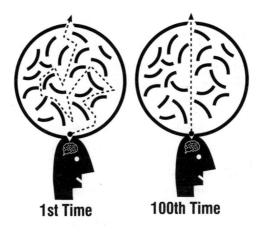

1st Time   **100th Time**

Figure 3.3   *Neural habit pathways building up*

Figure 3.4   *The critical voice*

helpful and supports what you are trying to achieve. If you do not give your brain a new message to focus on, it is likely to return to its old ways of thinking, not because it is useful or helpful, but simply because it is a comfortable habit.

EXERCISE 3.3 KEEP IT POSITIVE

Do you think more about the things you do not have as opposed to those things you have? Build up your positive patterns now by focusing your mind on all the things in your life you appreciate and for which you are thankful. This exercise will assist you in doing exactly this. List seven of the things you have in your life that you really appreciate.

1. _____
2. _____
3. _____
4. _____
5. _____
6. _____
7. _____

Now copy this list on to a small card that you can carry with you in your wallet or purse. Each time you are feeling down, or that your life is getting out of balance, take out your list and study the items, making them each come alive in your imagination. Keep updating this list.

As the first step to change is to become aware of your thoughts at given moments, use the Exercise 3.4 to identify what your thoughts might be when thinking about the situations detailed below. Change any negative thoughts to constructive thoughts that support your best performance in those situations.

EXERCISE 3.4 PROBLEM SITUATIONS

This exercise will help you to identify negative thought patterns and to change them to more helpful thinking patterns.

Situation	Negative thoughts	Helpful thinking
On your way to a meeting	Eg, this is going to be boring as usual	Eg, I can really see what I can get out of this by contributing more
When you are delegating		
When a team member gives you bad news		
When you have to give or receive feedback		
When under pressure from time and deadlines		
When giving a presentation		
When you arrive at your desk in the morning to open your mail and read your emails		

Having recorded these thoughts, spend a couple of minutes considering:

1. What influences from your past might have shaped this kind of thinking?
2. Is your thinking being driven by your own beliefs today or by these past influences?
3. Is this thinking helpful to you today?

LOSING SIGHT OF PERSPECTIVE

As well as negative thinking, it is possible to get into the habit of distorting your rational view of a situation and losing sight of perspective. This can be emphasized if you are under stress. Once again these distortions can affect both your ability to make decisions and to communicate effectively. Here are some examples:

1. Making sweeping statements. For example, one project fails and you think: 'Everything I do goes wrong.'
2. Focusing on the negative: only noticing and talking about negative experiences and missing the positive aspects of situations.
3. Taking things personally, even if the situation is beyond your control: 'I must have done something wrong', although there may have been many other factors involved.
4. Using generalizations such as 'never', 'everything', 'always', 'nothing', 'no one', regarding a specific situation.

Negative thinking and loss of perspective can sabotage your efforts to reach your goals and to work effectively. It skews your thinking. It has been proven, for example, that salespeople who think negatively sell fewer products. It therefore affects the bottom-line results of your work.

Start to become more aware of your thinking on an everyday basis and consider the rational nature of your current thinking. The following questions can be useful to challenge your thinking:

*   Just because this project has failed, why does it mean that 'everything I do goes wrong'?
*   Where can I find the good in this situation?
*   Even if this situation is difficult for me, what can I learn here?
*   Although I take responsibility for my part in this problem, what other

factors are influencing the situation?

- When I say something 'always' goes wrong, can I think of a time when it did not go wrong?
- Just because my boss/colleague thinks this is the 'right' way to do this job, does it mean that it is the 'only' way?
- Just because one person told me I am stupid, how does that make me stupid?
- Just because I made a mistake this time, does it follow that I am a failure?
- What is the worst that could happen? If the worst did happen, what resources do I have to manage that situation?
- Will this matter in three months' time or next year?

EXERCISE 3.5 THE RADIO

It can be difficult at first to learn new ways of thinking. Imagine your inner voice is a radio. It has a *Negative FM Channel*, a *Positive FM Channel* and a *Fanfare Music Channel*. As you become aware of negative thoughts, switch channels to the *Positive FM Channel*, and create positive and constructive thoughts in your head. These thoughts should be realistic and phrased in the positive continuous. For example: 'I am becoming more effective' or 'I am learning to think more creatively.'

There are, though, times when you may be unable to think of a positive replacement for a negative thought. Instead, you can invent a *Fanfare Music Channel*. Identify a piece of music that makes you feel good – it can be anything from opera to rap – and have that piece of music as your personal fanfare, always available to you on your imaginary radio. Music can touch human beings in a way that few other things do – an upbeat piece of music can make your spirits rise even on the gloomiest day.

The piece of music I shall call my fanfare is:

_____

_____

_____

Practise listening to *Positive FM* and the *Fanfare Music Channel* as often as you can.

Figure 3.5   *Positive FM*

PERFECTIONIST THINKING

Your thinking habits can sometimes result in perfectionism. This is when you develop rigid expectations of yourself and other people about how something should be done. This can be both irrational and can place unreasonable demands on yourself and those around you. 'Perfect' is a subjective concept: your idea of a perfect result or method of achieving something might be completely different to someone else's idea of perfect.

Perfectionism can also play havoc with deadlines, as perfectionists strive and strive to complete a job 'perfectly', taking longer than it needs or has been allocated to take. This can have an adverse impact on others, by breaking a deadline or causing others to be unable to progress in some way.

Antony, a senior manager we worked with, told us of his experience as a young man starting with a major publishing company. Working hard on a project, he was determined to 'get everything completely right', fearing that the project might otherwise fail. As he passed the project deadline his boss questioned his approach. He asked Antony to rate, on a scale of 0–10, his satisfaction level with the decisions he was making. Antony replied that he would give his decisions approximately 8 out of 10. The boss advised Antony to stop worrying about trying to get 10 out of 10 and get the job finished, remarking that new recruits must be allowed to make mistakes because mistakes are essential to growth and to learning. Mistakes, he said, are a sign that a person is pushing out the frontiers of knowledge and not getting paralysed by the fear of failure. Antony found this a valuable lesson. It enabled him to work faster and more creatively and to be content with 'excellent' rather than 'perfect'. When he himself became a senior manager, he continued this practice with his own staff.

Perfectionism is, indeed, a major barrier to creativity. Innovation comes through taking calculated risks and unsettling the status quo. Such a prospect can be extremely threatening to someone who wishes to do something 'perfectly'. A person may be so paralysed by the fear of failure that they take no action at all rather than taking action that may be 'wrong'. This can spell disaster for an organization trying to maintain its competitive edge and can also be frustrating for those working with such a person.

Communication with perfectionists can be exhausting. These people are driven to achieve and to reach their own impossibly high standards. Their inability to do so creates tension and frustration within themselves. It also creates tension with those who work with them. However hard you try, your efforts are never 'enough', and this can be demoralizing.

There is a subtle difference, as we hinted in the story about Antony, between perfectionism and the pursuit of excellence, where, whilst we strive for excellence, we recognize that we are all fallible and that mistakes occur.

People driven to be perfectionists use the words 'should', 'must' and 'ought' frequently in their language. They are also likely to use generalizations like 'never', 'nothing' and 'everything' and to lose sight of perspective.

People who are pursuing excellence use phrases such as 'I would prefer to' or 'let's try to achieve this result'. They can accept themselves if a project they are working on does not work out exactly as they would wish, although they strive to do it as well as is humanly possible.

Certain types of work demand perfect results. If you are working on building an aircraft, for example, 8 out of 10 would not be acceptable. Engineering projects, mathematical formulae, computer programming, etc are some other examples of work that demands a high degree of detailed 'perfection'. However, within this range there are still many options as to how you work and there may be other areas of your job in which you can question whether you are seeking a level of perfection that is limiting your creativity.

Consider your own approach in the following exercise:

EXERCISE 3.6 ARE YOU DRIVING YOURSELF AND OTHERS TOO HARD?

For each pair of statements, put a tick against the one which most appropriately describes you.

Driver	Enthusiast
You are driven by a fear of failure.	You are motivated by enthusiasm.
You perform tasks out of a sense of duty.	You enjoy the challenge of new tasks.
You are nervous about taking risks.	You enjoy taking risks and discovering more creative ways of working.
Your accomplishments, however great, never seem to satisfy you.	You get a sense of satisfaction from your efforts, even if they don't work as well as you would have liked.
The accomplishments of others are never good enough.	You accept that others are doing the best they can.
You feel your self-esteem depends on your achievements at work.	You feel you have intrinsic value in yourself, outside your achievements at work.
You think you must demonstrate your knowledge to impress people.	You feel accepted without trying to impress people.
If you do not achieve an important goal, you feel like a failure.	You realize that everyone makes mistakes occasionally and seek to learn from these experiences.
You think you must always be strong and not share your doubts and feelings.	You are not afraid of being vulnerable and sharing your feelings.
You judge others by your own view and methods of success.	You allow others to work to their best abilities in their own way.
You are late with deadlines because your work is not yet 'perfect enough'.	You know when a piece of work is 'good enough'.

If you scored more marks in the 'Driver' column, then consider whether your thoughts are putting adverse pressure on you and on those you work with. Look at your working habits and question whether you are limiting your creativity through this thinking. Look back and question whether deadlines have been missed as a result of your trying to get a 'perfect' result. Question whether in future 8 out of 10 might be acceptable in the circumstances. What are your comments on this?

_____

_____

_____

_____

_____

_____

In the business world you obviously need to strive for excellence. However, if this pursuit of excellence inspires an obsession for doing everything 'right', then you have to question whether this is limiting your ability to think creatively, to get a project in on time, or to work harmoniously with those around you. If this is the case, then question the way you are thinking about work and start to balance your perspective.

It can be helpful to ask for feedback and advice from colleagues. Feedback provides new insights into how you might look at a situation. It is always possible to look at things from a different viewpoint, and constructive feedback related to your desired objective will give you more choices regarding your own approach.

Developing new ways of thinking gives you options and a greater sense of personal control. Instead of feeling victim to a set of circumstances at work, you can choose to think in a way that supports your own ability to manage yourself effectively within those circumstances. Like the age-old saying of seeing 'a glass half-empty or a glass half-full', you can learn to focus on the positive simply by switching the signal from one neural pathway to another. You can, quite literally, rewire the neural circuitry of your brain.

Many of the senior managers we work with comment that it is frequently difficult to get people to share their ideas for fear of having the 'wrong' thought, or of looking stupid. These fears seriously limit creativity. As you learn to value your unique contribution, you can celebrate the fact that, even if others do not always agree with your thoughts, it is likely that your approach will stimulate them to think differently about the problem in hand.

In terms of contribution at work, it is important to realize that no one in your organization – or, indeed, the world – will have the same set of thoughts and ideas as you. If you do not share those thoughts, your co-workers and your business may be deprived of your contribution. This is particularly important as you begin to consider yourself as a 'brand'. It is part of what is known as your USP or 'unique selling proposal'. Your thinking is a key factor in your marketability and your success.

In this chapter you have discovered that you are in control of your thinking. Indeed, although it may not seem that way when you are under pressure, your thoughts actually represent a true area of freedom, as, whatever happens in your external world, you do, in fact, have the option to choose your response through the way you think.

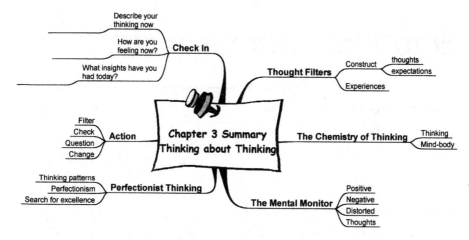

Figure 3.6 *Summary: thinking about thinking*

4

Emotional Intelligence

In the Five-Step Thinking System (see page 17, above), we demonstrated that your beliefs influence your thoughts and your thoughts influence your emotions. In this chapter, you will discover for yourself the connection between thoughts and emotions and how you can learn to manage them. The advent and acceptance of emotional intelligence, largely inspired by Daniel Goleman's book, *Emotional Intelligence*, published in 1996, may well have been a breakthrough for what has long been a stepchild topic.

In the business world of recent years the emphasis on technology has led to a somewhat intolerant attitude towards this subject. There is often an inclination to pretend that there is no place for emotions in the workplace. The result is that people are treated as if they were machines. However, we see examples of emotional behaviour every day at work and emotions are an integral part of what it is to be human.

How aware are you of the emotions you are experiencing at work? For example, a survey identified public speaking, a common event in business, as the number one universal fear across the world. How often do you feel nervous before a presentation or meeting, or when giving bad news to a colleague or client?

Consider some of the meetings you have attended where people have been too nervous to express an opinion, or where someone became angry.

Consider the feelings you have during a difficult telephone call. Consider also the feeling of excitement when you win a new client or are enjoying the challenge of a new project.

Your emotions can motivate or demotivate you and result in helping or hindering your work performance. You can learn to manage them and become 'emotionally intelligent'. First, however, you must learn to become *aware* of them. The next few exercises help you to develop a greater understanding of your own responses and of the connection between your thoughts and your feelings.

EXERCISE 4.1 MOTIVATORS AND DEMOTIVATORS

To identify the key work factors that stimulate pleasurable feelings, complete the branch 'motivators' on Figure 4.1 and add more if appropriate. For example, 'I am motivated by getting the job done.' As with the previous MindManager map exercise, add a single word or short phrase on top of each line. Then consider the factors that inspire negative feelings and add these to the 'demotivators' branch. Take two to three minutes to complete this exercise on the map.

Then complete this sentence: I am happiest at work when

_____

_____

_____

Figure 4.1   *Motivators and demotivators*

By identifying the key factors that you enjoy doing at work, you will improve your work performance. Ask yourself: 'Are there more of these activities I can incorporate into my present job?'

Now complete this sentence: My emotions interfere with my work performance when

_____

_____

_____

An IT manager in an international organization was having severe difficulties with the noise levels in the open-plan office in which he had to work. It was affecting his performance, as his work was highly detailed. He arranged a meeting with his supervisor to discuss his problems but felt that his requests were not adequately understood and became angry. His supervisor chastised him that it was 'not professional' to display anger in this way. The next day the same IT manager was amused to hear his supervisor raising his voice with another colleague and slamming his office door loudly as the colleague left.

This demonstrates that executives can try to deny their emotions in order to appear 'professional'. It also demonstrates that emotions exist in the workplace as much as they do elsewhere. Getting in touch with your emotions is the first step to emotional intelligence and puts you in touch with your thinking.

EXERCISE 4.2 EMOTIONAL MANAGEMENT IN BUSINESS

Evaluate how effective you are in business situations at:	Weak	Needs developing	Acceptable	Good	Excellent
1. Know what you are feeling	1	2	3	4	5
2. Know why you are feeling it	1	2	3	4	5
3. Managing your emotions	1	2	3	4	5
4. Controlling your temper	1	2	3	4	5
5. Following your intuition	1	2	3	4	5
6. Knowing what you want	1	2	3	4	5
7. Avoiding conflict	1	2	3	4	5
8. Expressing your needs	1	2	3	4	5
9. Accepting your emotions	1	2	3	4	5
10. Managing emotions under pressure	1	2	3	4	5

If you have scored 40 or more, this indicates that you have a good understanding of how to manage yourself. If you have scored less than 40, then use this first section of the book to tune into the thoughts behind your emotions.

Consider different ways of thinking about situations and see if it affects your emotions. If a thought is stimulating negative emotions then challenge your thoughts and notice if your feelings change. For example, if you are thinking 'I can't stand the noise in this office', try thinking 'I can manage to focus on my work despite the noise'. When standing on a bus or train we are often able to tune into a book. We can use that same capacity to tune into work in an open-plan environment. It is a matter of mental focus and practice.

Your thinking affects your emotional state. You are often attempting to move away from pain and towards pleasure. However, the contradiction to this is that risk-taking, an essential part of creativity, does involve a certain amount of discomfort in order to be successful. This would account for why a certain amount of stress is healthy. The key is to find the balance that suits you. Think back over some of the major decisions in your life and ask yourself what part emotion played in them:

EXERCISE 4.3 DECISION-MAKER

1. Buying your first car.
2. Buying your first home.
3. Choosing a business partner.
4. A major business deal.
5. A change in career.
6. Moving to a new city or country.
7. Making a major investment with your own money.
8. Deciding to get married.
9. Deciding on a course of study at a college or university.
10. Discovering a strategic business plan is flawed and informing your superiors.

Consider whether logical analysis came first in your decision chain or whether the feeling you experienced inspired you to develop the rational arguments necessary to acquire what you wanted emotionally. As adults we are often trained only to listen to logic and reason and forget that emotions are themselves a form of personal intelligence. As emotions are processed through the limbic area of your brain closely linked to memory, there is evidence to suggest that your feelings develop from your personal experiences of life and are therefore giving you valuable information. See Figure 4.2.

The basis of the Five-Step Thinking Model is to demonstrate that if you change your thinking you can learn to manage your emotions. The thoughts and expectations you have of a situation drive your emotions. For example, if you expect that your boss should give you a day off when you ask for one, you may well feel extremely disappointed if he or she does not do so. The action has not come up to your expectation of your desired outcome, so you feel upset.

Similarly, if you are making a presentation to a prospective client and expect that you must perform perfectly because you believe that otherwise the client will not give you the job, you are likely to feel extremely anxious. If, on the other hand, your expectation is that you will do the best that you can – ie, pursue excellence rather than perfection – and have an expectation that, even if you do not get a job from this client, you will get one from another client, you are likely to feel calmer.

These thoughts and expectations have a direct effect on your feelings. Therefore by changing our thoughts and expectations we can change our feelings.

Use Exercise 4.4 to explore your expectations and the emotions you experienced in a recent situation.

Figure 4.2 *Emotional intelligence*

THE ABCDE THINKING MODEL

This powerful model, originally developed by Dr Albert Ellis, President of the Albert Ellis Institute for Rational Emotive Behaviour Therapy, New York, will enable you:

1. to become aware of your thoughts and emotions (ABC, as below);
2. to dispute your own response to the situation (D); and
3. if appropriate, to exchange your old thoughts and replace them with more supportive inner-voice messages (E).

In this model, ABCDE stands for the following:

- A stands for the Activating event.
- B stands for the Belief or expectation you have of yourself, other people and/or the situation in general.
- C stands for the Consequential emotion.
- D stands for Disputing your response. Here you dispute your response to the situation in three different ways:
    (1) Is it logical?
    (2) Would everyone take the same viewpoint?
    (3) Is it helpful to you?
- E stands for Exchange your thinking with more constructive thoughts.

Study the following example, before completing Exercise 4.4.

- A Activating event: lack of time re deadline.
- B Belief: eg, 'I will never do this in time', 'I am no good if I don't manage to finish perfectly', 'My boss should not have done this to me', or 'There is not enough time'.
- C Consequence: fear and stress.
- D Dispute:
    (1) Just because it is preferable that you manage to meet the deadline, is it logical to believe that you *must*? What law of the universe says that you must?
    (2) What is the evidence that everyone in this situation would manage to meet the deadline?
    (3) How is it helpful to you to believe that you *must* manage and that you are no good if you don't?
- E Exchange: what would be a more helpful way of thinking? Eg, 'It would be preferable if I manage but I can still accept myself if I don't', 'I have enough time to do the best I can'.

Negative thinking affects your performance. Watch generalizations and over-dramatic responses to a situation. 'Enough', for example, is a subjective word. What does not feel 'enough' time to you, may be 'enough' time for someone else, or vice versa. You are more likely to reach your deadline if you remain calm and think clearly, pursuing excellence rather than perfection.

Please complete the following exercise.

EXERCISE 4.4 ABCDE MODEL

What follows demonstrates the close relationship between emotions and thoughts. How have you faced up to these? Write down:

A: A challenging situation you faced, preferably at work. Try to take a specific recent incident.

_____

_____

_____

A Activating event

B Belief or expectation

C Consequential emotion

D Disputing your response

E Exchange your thinking

Figure 4.3 *The ABCDE Thinking Model*

B: What beliefs, thoughts and expectations were you holding of yourself, other people and/or the situation in general.

(1) Of yourself (eg, 'I should/must...):

_____

_____

_____

(2) Of other people involved (eg, the other people should have...'):

_____

_____

_____

(3) Of the situation in general (eg, meetings should adhere to the agenda...):

_____

_____

_____

C: The emotion you experienced when you faced this challenge:

_____

_____

_____

D: When you look at the thoughts and expectations listed in B, ask yourself whether or not they were rational and helpful to you. You can do this by disputing your thinking in the following way:

(1) Just because, in your construction of an ideal situation, you would prefer the situation to be this way, is it logical to believe that it *must* be that way?

_____

_____

_____

(2) Would other people all respond to this situation in the same way?

_____

_____

_____

(3) Was your thinking actually helping you to achieve your desired goal?

_____

_____

_____

E: (1) How might you prefer to think if you experienced this situation again?

_____

_____

_____

_____

_____

_____

(2) What can you learn from how other people might respond to this situation?

_____

_____

_____

_____

_____

(3) How might changing your thinking affect your feelings?

_____

_____

_____

_____

_____

(4) How else might you learn to respond in future?

_____

_____

_____

_____

_____

_____

_____

_____

By aligning your expectations to realistic and achievable goals of excellence, considering the time available, resources and acceptable standards of quality, you can now develop constructive emotions that support you.

EMOTIONAL INTELLIGENCE

By becoming aware of your thoughts, you can begin to manage your emotions. If you have a tendency to perfectionist thinking you may well be more stressed than someone who is willing to make a few mistakes. Become more attuned to your feelings. By heeding early warning signals of how you are feeling you can manage the consequences of these emotions.

There are many examples of people who are 'hijacked' by emotions they did not acknowledge at an early stage. Incidents of 'road rage', violence or people storming out of a meeting are events you may have experienced. People can also become ill. One example of this was when we were working with a police force and were told about a constable who, some years earlier, had witnessed a terrible crash on a motorway, in which he had watched a driver of a van burn to death and was unable to reach him. At that time the police force were less aware of the long-term effects of witnessing horrific incidents and the constable had completed his duty, attending to the needs of other drivers and interviewing survivors. He had no debriefing session regarding his own emotions. Some time later there was another multiple accident and the same police officer was called to the scene. As he approached the crash, he stopped and was unable to respond to the call-out as the fear of witnessing a similar scene became too much to bear. He had to take leave and was eventually given early retirement from the force. The rescue services are now much more aware of the dangerous effects of covering up or denying emotions and full debriefing is given at the time of such incidents.

Fortunately, few of us are exposed to this kind of tragic incident. However, even smaller events in your life can revisit you at a later time if you do not listen and attend to your own emotional needs. Although emotions are natural, and the appropriate expression of them is helpful, being overwhelmed by them is generally unhelpful in the workplace.

Now that you have begun to understand more about your emotions, it is time to take an in-depth look at what it means to be 'emotionally intelligent'.

THE EMOTIONAL INTELLIGENCE MODEL

1. Knowing what you feel – learning and staying with your feelings long enough to identify your emotion. 'When I am frightened I feel tension in my neck. It is OK to feel frightened.'
2. Knowing why you feel it – whether the feeling is based on a belief, an expectation, past experience, imagination or a situation you face. 'This emotion is the result of my imagination as I am worrying about being made redundant, but this has not actually happened to me.'
3. Acknowledging your emotion – 'Yes, I do feel angry.'
4. Expressing your feelings openly, honestly and appropriately. Sharing your feelings responsibly – 'When you do that I feel upset.'
5. Knowing how to manage yourself and how to help yourself to feel better. 'I can handle this situation by changing my thinking and taking the required action.'

The models introduced in this book are designed to help you to manage your emotions.

Memory can also help you access good feelings. The following memory exercise will assist you to access pleasurable emotions.

EXERCISE 4.5 REMEMBERING THE PAST

1. Consider three moments in your life when you felt particularly happy. List them on the MindManager Map and describe each incident and situation in a few words.

2. When you have completed the map, stop and think about those times. You can use your memory to bring back the sensations of happiness. Memory works through the five senses, as this is where information comes into your brain. In any situation you experience, your five senses are alert

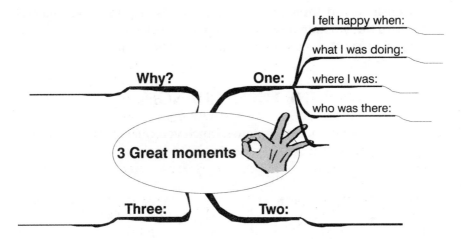

Figure 4.4 *Three great moments*

and absorbing information into your memory bank. It is therefore possible to revive those feelings again through concentrating on the memory of an experience.

3. When you consider these three moments in your life, can you find any themes or ingredients that are common to all three?

_____

_____

_____

If so, how might you incorporate these ingredients into your life more often? Write on Figure 4.4 what aspects of each experience you would like most to remember and incorporate.

There are numerous ways in which you can begin to bring more plea-surable emotions into your everyday worklife. There are many hints about this in this book. Here are some suggestions to help you.

THREE EMOTIONALLY INTELLIGENT INTERVENTIONS

1. Use the ABCDE model to identify and change your thinking to support you.

2. Get creative and think of as many methods as possible to help you improve the situation physically and emotionally.
3. Experiment with new ways of thinking and behaving.

THE THREE CHANGES

There are three immediate techniques which you can tap into and address strong emotions:

1. Changing your Thinking;
2. Changing your Physiology; and
3. Changing the Circumstances in which you find yourself.

Let us examine each of these in turn.

TECHNIQUE 1: CHANGING YOUR THINKING

How easy it is to get bogged down in a problem! Often people fall into a pattern of negative discussion regarding a situation or a person at work

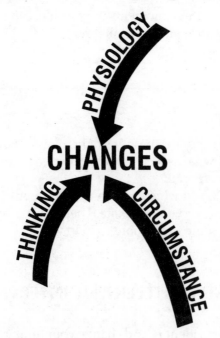

Figure 4.5 *The Three Changes Process*

(we discuss this in further detail in Chapter 10, 'Working Relationships'). A new phrase that has been coined in the UK is 'blamestorming', where people look for someone to blame for the situation in which they find themselves. Is it not uncommon to hear the accusation 'It is the management's fault!'

Much as it can be helpful to share experiences and get support, the sharing and berating are unlikely to alter the factors influencing that situation. It is extremely important, therefore, to consider what changes you would like to experience.

Emotional intelligence means taking personal responsibility for the situation in which you find yourself and devising active remedial solutions. There will be some situations that you cannot change. However, you can change the way you look at it. This next Inner Modelling technique helps you focus on a positive result.

OVER TO YOU

Outcome – decide upon it and make it positive (what would you like to happen?)
Visualize – your successful goal (what would it look like if you got there?)
Emotional check – enthusiasm factor (if you had this tomorrow, would you really want it?)
Review methods – analyse your methods to reach your outcome (how can you get there?)
Try – first steps (what is the first thing you can do?)
Observe – your thoughts and make them constructive (is your thinking supporting you?)
You – can make some mistakes (are you learning from different methods?)
Observe – review and adjust methods and goals (how else could you do this?)
Upwards – and onwards: success is a continuous process!

Keep this acronym in your emotional intelligence toolbox, for the next time you have a problem and need to focus your mind on the positive outcome.

Visualization can be a powerful technique as it enables you to influence your brain into thinking you have already achieved your goal by building up pictures and sensations of what it will be like when you get there. This helps you to change your emotions by imagining the confident or exhilarated feeling associated with that achievement. Positive visual imagination sends signals from your visual cortex that change your biochemistry to release endorphins into your system. Endorphins are associated with pleasurable feelings.

Therefore, if you are experiencing a difficult situation at work, create an imagined video of yourself gradually feeling better every day. Build up pictures, thoughts and feelings in your mind of how your life at work might improve. Think of this as often as possible as it will develop the neural networks in your brain to support your actions.

Make sure that your language also supports your goal. Sometimes fear of failure influences people to talk negatively or dismissively of the thing they want to achieve. For example, you hear people saying 'I'll never learn to speak French', although their goal is to speak French because they are being transferred to an office in France. Align your language, therefore, to your goals, as this supports your thinking. It also gives clear signals to those around you about the goals you are working towards and they may be able to help and support you.

Your mind is your tool for managing your emotions. Through memory, imagination and changing your thoughts to support your goals, you can enjoy more positive experiences every day even if the circumstances themselves cannot be changed.

TECHNIQUE 2: CHANGING YOUR PHYSIOLOGY

Your body has an intelligence of its own that signals to you when you are not listening to your emotions closely enough. Notice physical symptoms. What are they trying to tell you?

Altering your physical position can, in itself, improve your emotional state. For example, if you notice that your shoulders are hunched and you are stooping, try shaking your neck and shoulders a little and standing more upright. Feel your spine go straight, your shoulders go back a little and your lungs expand. Stand a little taller each day, not stiffly but in a relaxed way, lengthening your spine, softening your shoulders and opening your lungs. This simple action can help you to feel better even in the midst of a difficult situation. Try this now. See Figure 4.6.

TECHNIQUE 3: CHANGING THE CIRCUMSTANCES

What actions could you take to change situations that are stimulating negative emotions? Sometimes, a simple action will help you manage yourself. The courage required to make changes can, in itself, stimulate your self-esteem.

Figure 4.6   *Listen to your body*

Changing the circumstances can be as simple as moving your desk into a different position, or improving your filing system. Small things like this can improve your emotional state. It could alternatively involve quite large changes, such as moving office or job, or starting your own business.

CHUNK YOUR GOALS

Chunk your goals into manageable steps, as this will help you to manage your emotions. An entrepreneur we work alongside had been excited and yet nervous about starting her own business. She had not appreciated that the business would evolve and grow over a period of time. It would not suddenly become a massive organization. At the outset she had been fearful that she would be expected to be the accomplished managing director immediately. In fact, when she broke the goals down to one step at a time, she realized she could develop herself slowly alongside the development of the business. This eased the anxious emotions she had previously experienced.

TUNING INTO YOUR INTUITION

Another route to emotional intelligence is to tune into your intuition. Most of us have an intuitive faculty that can affect our emotions and responses.

No doubt you have experienced a time when you 'knew' a particular person would telephone you, and perhaps another time when you 'knew' that there would be a space to park your car around the next corner.

Your body also gives you intuitive signals. There are times when you may have a negative feeling about something or someone but cannot rationalize it. This may be experienced as tension in the shoulders or stomach. Become attuned to these signals. At other times you may suddenly feel a sense of excitement without being able to rationalize why. Notice it and watch out to see if something nice comes your way. If it does, learn to recognize that symptom and signal again for the future. These represent your own positive and negative intuitive warning systems.

Intuition is an area of your emotional intelligence and is thought to be derived from the experiences you have had in your life. You are often too absorbed in daily activities to notice these signals, although they can provide useful information, especially when making decisions. Take time to tune in.

THE WAY AHEAD

You may experience some discomfort as you become aware of your emotions and start to develop your own methods of managing them. It may be that you have gone to lengths to avoid tapping into certain emotions. Indeed, many people at work believe this is the 'mature' way to deal with emotions.

However, as we said earlier, if you want to avoid being hijacked by your emotions it is best to listen to them and deal with them chunk by chunk as you progress through life. Any discomfort you might feel is a healthy sign that you are trying to think and respond differently. If you experience no discomfort, this may indicate that you are using the same formula as before. However, seek support or professional advice if the discomfort becomes difficult to handle yourself.

To move forward we need to change the focus of our thoughts. These in turn alter our emotions and drive new actions. Measure your progress. Notice which events and activities give you negative emotions and which support your positive enjoyment of work. A recent survey in the UK reinforced the fact that people in business now expect to enjoy their work. If you are not enjoying your work, you are unlikely to be working to your full potential. If this is the case, it is worth using the rest of this book to focus your mind and your actions on goals to help you find a way to enjoy your present job. Alternatively it is possible that you might perform better in another area of work and you can explore options as you read on.

There may be setbacks along your path but you are starting a journey towards feeling more powerful and in control. Stay in touch with your feelings as you progress through this book and at the same time keep focused on your positive outcomes. In the next chapter, you will discover that your ability to change your emotional response will affect your behaviour and improve your ability to reach your goals.

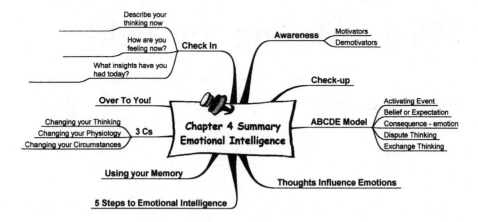

Figure 4.7 *Summary: emotional intelligence*

5

What's Making You Tick?

What is 'behaviour'? A dictionary definition is 'conduct, bearing, manners'. It is, therefore, *how* you do something rather than *what* you do. In our Five-Step Thinking Model, you discovered that your behaviour is shaped by your values, thoughts and emotions. If you are feeling good you will behave confidently. If you are feeling sad you will behave less confidently. You may still do the same task and still do that task competently, but behaviour lies in that intangible area that relates to the energy you create in completing the task.

If the task is done properly either way, does it matter how you do it? If you are questioning this, consider what it is like to work with someone who is enthusiastic, compared to someone who is miserable. Or, if a person is reliable or unreliable, that person may complete the required task but their unreliability can create a lack of trust in fellow team members. This lack of trust eventually impairs the team's performance. Behaviours affect the morale of a whole organization.

We asked several senior executives in a variety of professions – bankers, lawyers, traders, health managers, and entrepreneurs – what they regarded as the key ingredients they brought to their job. The responses included:

- team player
- quick
- responsive
- positive
- encouraging of others
- brave
- self-confident
- open
- resilient
- good learner
- good teacher
- creative
- results-driven
- competitive
- resilient
- multi-faceted

- imaginative
- fun
- reliable
- motivated
- enthusiastic
- inspirational
- committed
- dynamic
- congruent
- visionary
- persuasive
- adaptable
- flexible
- persistent
- self-knowing
- intuitive

You may notice that there are no skill-sets in this list. Out of ten adjectives there was only an average of one mention of any skill-set per person asked. In some cases no skills were listed. Put one skilled lawyer next to another skilled lawyer and the difference lies in the behaviours described above. The secret to your peak performance lies in your behaviour.

EXERCISE 5.1 BEHAVIOUR CHECK

1. Look at the list of words above and tick the five that most apply to you when you think of the key ingredients you bring to your work. If you have any further words that you would prefer to those already listed, make a new list in the space below.

_____

_____

_____

_____

_____

_____

2. Now tick or add another five that you would like to add to your daily behaviour.

_____

_____

_____

_____

_____

3. Consider how situations influence your behaviour. Are you results-driven in projects? Are you imaginative in the methods you use to approach your work? Are you a team player all the time or are there some situations in which you find it easier to work as a team? Situations and Behaviours:

SITUATION	BEHAVIOUR

Having looked at yourself and some of your habitual behaviours, consider what helps you to perform at your peak. For example, some people feel validated and inspired by making a decision that reflects integrity even if it does not yield the best bottom-line result. Other people would feel validated and inspired by getting the bottom-line result, whatever the means.

It takes some courage to look at yourself honestly, but the key to self-knowledge is learning to recognize and accept yourself as you are. Not accepting all the parts to you, good and bad, tends to set up an inner conflict and denial that can impair performance.

Every person alive has some facets that they would not boast about. We are all, at times, jealous, greedy, selfish, etc. There are some situations that inspire the worst in you and other situations that inspire the best in you. You have already begun, in Exercise 4.1, to consider the situations that bring out some of your better qualities. Use this next exercise to consider the situations that inspire your best and worst behaviour. These may be situations or they may be people, or they may be your own doubts or fantasies.

EXERCISE 5.2 THE BEHAVIOUR CHAIN

Consider yourself now in the circle of your colleagues and complete the map. Consider what inspires your best and worst behaviours.

Then consider if you could bring out the best in yourself more often. Your own behaviour and attitudes not only affect the quality of your life but also the quality of the lives of the people around you.

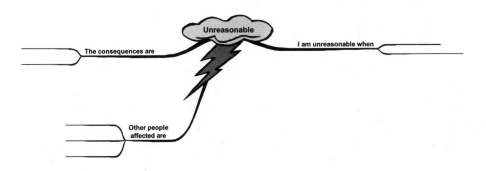

Figure 5.1 *'I am unreasonable when'*

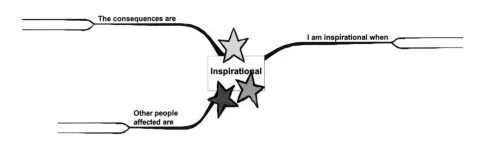

Figure 5.2 *'I am inspirational when'*

If there are any action points you would like to set for yourself from these exercises, use the space below to jot them down.

_____

_____

_____

Have you copied the behaviour of your own influential role models without questioning them? For example:

- If you have difficulty managing money, did your parents also have difficulty?   yes / no
- Has your career path in any way reflected that of your role models?   yes / no
- Are your exercise or dietary habits similar to those of your role models?   yes / no
- Do your relationship behaviours reflect those of your role models?   yes / no

Have you found that the corporate culture in which you work has influenced you to behave in a 'company' way in order to gain acceptance and the likelihood of promotion? When you question this, check whether this behaviour reflects the values and beliefs you developed in Chapter 2. The more you are able to align your beliefs with your behaviours at work, the more likely you are to be contributing your full energy and potential in your career, not adapting yourself to other people's values and expectations.

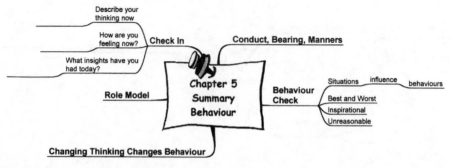

Figure 5.3 *Summary: behaviour*

A critical factor in leadership is the role model you present to those who rely on you for direction and guidance. As a leader you need to examine your thinking processes and behaviours and understand that your past experiences need not be a determinant of your future. In this way you do a service not only to yourself but also to those to whom you provide leadership.

6

Actions Speak Louder Than Words

The final step in The Five-Step Thinking Model is that of Action. All of us can look back at actions that have changed our lives for the better or worse. Taking action results in concrete memories and forms major learning points throughout your life. They are *what* you do. Actions can be seen and experienced and, more importantly, they have consequences as they follow the law of cause and effect.

EXERCISE 6.1 ACTION REVIEW

In Exercise 1.6, you drew a picture to represent your career path. Either return to that picture or use the space below to draw a line to represent your life. Mark on this line some of the major actions that you have taken in your life. Examples might be moving home, getting married, starting in a profession, your first job, applying for promotion, writing an article, taking action to change something that would move you ahead.

_____

_____

_____

_____

_____

_____

What can you discover from re-examining these actions in the light of how you want to direct and change your life in the future? Write, draw or doodle your thoughts in the space below.

Reflect upon some of the major decisions you have made that led to actions. Consider whether you had a deliberate chain of events that led you to where you now stand. Fill in the space below.

Did you find it difficult to think about some of the actions you have taken? Perhaps they did not result in what you wanted. However, it is too easy to focus on regret and not solutions. One of the factors of being human is that we spend much of our time thinking about what we might do in the future, and regretting what we did or did not do in our past, missing the moment.

Taking action, even if the result is contrary to expectation, is a sign of courage. As Theodore Roosevelt once commented:

> *'It is not the critic who counts; nor the man who points out where the strong man stumbled or where the doer of deeds could have done better. The credit belongs to the man who is actually in the arena whose face is marred, with dust, and sweat and blood. At best he knows the triumph of high achievement; if he fails, at least he fails while daring greatly; so that his place shall never be with those cold and timid souls who knew neither victory nor defeat.'*

The actions you have taken may have marred your face with dust here and there but if you had risked nothing you would have had few events to learn from. If you think back to the 'Over To You' model (see page 61, above) you will remember that you need to review your methods and goals continually and accept that successes and failures are merely feedback to your goal.

Consider the process of driving a bicycle towards a set destination. As you go along the road, you are constantly adjusting and readjusting the handlebars to keep as direct a route as possible towards your destination. If you did not adjust along your route you would not be prepared to meet unexpected bumps in the road, or corners you were not previously aware existed. You may over-compensate once or twice, but you generally reach your goal through this constant adjustment.

Figure 6.1 *The constant adjustments and readjustments in life*

In this context you do not regard these adjustments as 'failures'. They are successful survival techniques. You keep your eyes alert for obstacles and generally feel content to respond flexibly to whatever comes your way. At work, however, people can sometimes become fearful of making mistakes. In Chapter 3, 'Thinking About Thinking', you discovered how a fear of failure can paralyse and remove the ability to respond to new challenges. If you were too rigid as you rode a bicycle, you might be thrown into the ditch by an unexpected stone in the road. Think of how a cat rights itself when it falls from a tree, or think how much more likely skiers would be to hurt themselves if they were tense when they fell. A degree of suppleness and flexibility of thought enables us to take action and not be paralysed into inaction.

One major problem we notice in the organizations with whom we work is the frustration of inaction. In our client surveys, only a small percentage of meetings result in action. People may agree verbally to do something but by the next meeting often nothing has been done. Then again in companies where downsizing has occurred, people take little or no action in fear of losing their jobs.

Think back to occasions where you or your colleagues committed to do something but never got round to it. Inaction, or procrastination, tends to diminish personal self-esteem and also to demotivate a team. Each time someone says they will do something and does not do it, a fraction of trust is removed. On the contrary, if someone takes the required action, this step ripples further than the individual and can inspire others. Even if the action fails, a certain energy is set up within the group.

EXERCISE 6.2 ACTIONS OUTSTANDING

Use Figure 6.2 to consider any outstanding actions you or your team have committed to do but have not yet achieved. Set times and details to prompt you to take action now.

When considering the subject of action and inaction, remind yourself that your own responses will be reflecting your own attitude to action and influencing trust within your circle of colleagues and clients. Each time you do what you said you would, you are enhancing your brand image and maintaining your own marketability within your present job. You are also sending positive signals to those around you who may be able to offer you a promotion or new work.

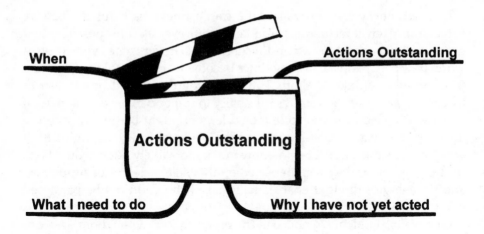

When

Actions Outstanding

Actions Outstanding

What I need to do

Why I have not yet acted

Figure 6.2 *'Actions outstanding'*

ACTIONS IN TIME

One of our most precious resources is that of time. There never appears to be enough time to do all the things you want to do and each day unfolds as a race against the clock. Your activities can be broken down into three major time segments.

1. work: this for many of us is self-explanatory;
2. maintenance: these are all the things we need to do to keep both ourselves and our family units in working order (eg, grocery shopping, driving to work, housekeeping, administering our personal affairs); and
3. leisure activities, which incorporates recreations, sports, hobbies, movies and dining out.

These three dimensions of life into which our activities may be categorized can be visually portrayed as in Figure 6.3.

EXERCISE 6.3 HOW WE SPEND OUR TIME

In this exercise you are asked to rate your real percentages in these three categories in Circle A (Figure 6.4) and what would be your ideal percentages in Circle B (Figure 6.5). As we know, the importance of life is

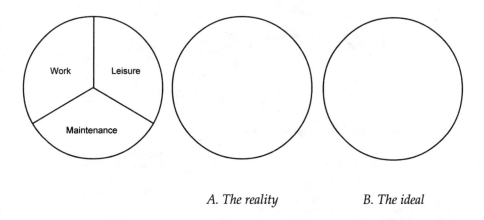

A. *The reality*   B. *The ideal*

Figure 6.3   *How we spend our time*

balance, which results in happiness. If your Circle A is not aligned to your Circle B you need to start thinking of ways to change this equation.

The art of prioritization is crucial in today's fast-moving business world. It is easy to have your attention diverted by a telephone call, or someone passing your desk for advice with a problem. In order to make good decisions about the actions you need to take at work, it is advisable to consider the key ingredients of your job. Why are you employed? What skills or qualities are you employed for? If you are self-employed, what are your main strengths?

EXERCISE 6.4 UNLOCKING TIME

Consider your time pressures and how they impact on your actions and jot down any thoughts on Figure 6.4.

A perception of lack of time can pressurize you into taking impulsive actions or it can disempower you from taking any action at all! It is important to obtain a sense of control over your time and, in making decisions, to prioritize your key tasks. You will find more detail on this in Chapter 16, 'A Balanced Approach', but at this stage consider how the passing of time can vary despite the fact that there are only so many hours in a day. Think about how slowly time can pass when you are waiting for a

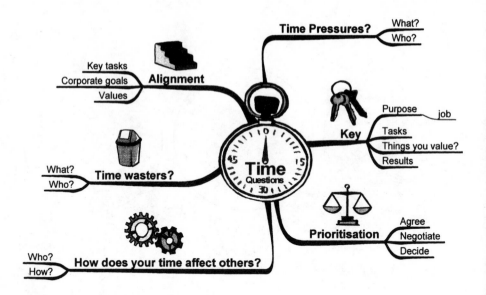

Figure 6.4 *MindManager Map on 'The time padlock'*

prospective client to phone you; think how fast time can pass when you have a great deal of work to do. Once again, through the Five-Step Thinking Model you can come to think differently about time and this will help you to manage it.

LIFE BALANCE

The next question is a more detailed analysis of your satisfaction level with your life.

EXERCISE 6.5 MY LIFE

Figure 6.5 illustrates a suggested overview of life activities. You may wish to add more, or to change some of the items displayed on the branches to suit your lifestyle.

1. Insert your assessment of your satisfaction level on a scale of 0–10 on each branch of Figure 6.5.

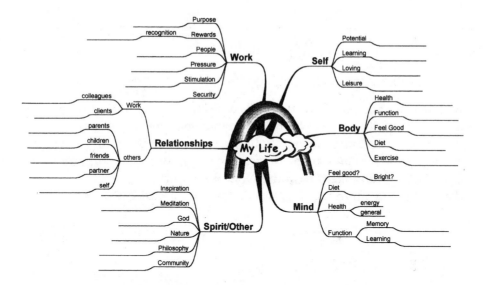

Figure 6.5 *MindManager Map on 'My life'*

2. In future I wish to focus more of my time on:

_____

_____

_____

This exercise identifies areas of your life that you would like to work on more fully. In order to create balance you will need to take new actions.

Now that you have learnt more about the Five-Step Thinking Model, you will be able to understand how both your thoughts and emotions determine your actions. Change your thinking to the positive continuous verb when you set yourself action goals, as this gives a signal to your brain that you are starting to do those things which you would like to do. For example, 'I am exercising at the gym after work', 'I am reading one business book a week', or 'I am writing an article for the company newsletter by Friday'.

EXERCISE 6.6 BRAINSET 'ACTION'

Practise writing actions you want to do in the near future and start a new brain pattern:

_____

_____

_____

Both balance and positive action will contribute to your overall good image and productivity at work. It enhances your self-esteem and creates confidence. Being in control of your thoughts, emotions and actions enables you to radiate success and keep abreast of change. Each thought and action builds your brand identity in the workplace. In the next section you will discover how your thoughts and actions are influencing your life.

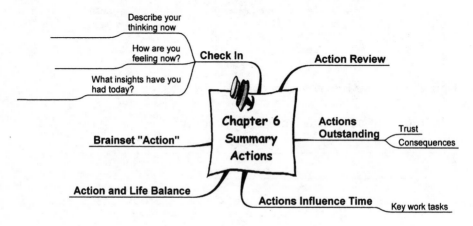

Figure 6.6 *Summary: actions*

PART TWO

WHO IS NAVIGATING?

7

Your Success Story

Certain influences have shaped your past but it is important to realize that you are the creative force behind all you have achieved to date. You are navigating, whether you fully realize it or not. Experiences, people and events will be contributing to your success but it is your response to these experiences that make the difference. You are the sum total of the choices and actions you have been taking up until this moment. In the day-to-day events of life it is easy to overlook this fact and to lose focus of where you want to go or how you are going to get there. It is easy to become side-tracked by problems that need immediate attention.

Success breeds success. If you are not aware of your own success story then there is no seed from which to breed more success. Failure also breeds success. Think also about the times that you have learnt and grown from mistakes or turned bad situations into good. It is essential to recognize and value your own capabilities. They have helped you to reach distant goals, have cushioned you from buffeting waves, have kept you on track in the midst of storms, and have motivated you through calm or tedious times.

Think back over your working life and you will discover a series of events that have led to your moments of personal success, no matter how insignificant these may appear to you now. Because these events are stored in your long-term memory and not something you are conscious of every day, it is easy to forget your successes and your strengths and discount your ability to overcome present obstacles. Few people are taught how to assess fully the strength of their personal life and work experiences, or take the time to do so.

The majority of people we have interviewed and worked with around the world agree that they realize they are the creative force in their lives. As human beings we have the power to imagine different ways of working and living. We have the power to create new products and services. We have used this power, consciously or unconsciously, to reach this point and can now use it to create more of what we want in our lives.

In fact the human brain thrives on challenges and obstacles. It is a success mechanism and works ceaselessly to find the right formula, thriving on solving problems. Without this capability you would not be where you are today. This next exercise will assist you in your ability to recognize your strengths and to use them as a springboard for further success.

EXERCISE 7.1 YOUR TALENT BANK

1. On Figure 7.1, add in as many as you can of the following:

- Background and life experiences: Where do you come from? Where were you brought up? Are you the eldest, middle or youngest of your family, etc? Have you travelled a lot? Think about your life experiences, good and bad, that have shaped and strengthened you and given you skills.
- Learning and skills: What are your work, educational and life skills (such as academic qualifications, work learning, training, and outside work skills such as cooking, driving, painting, DIY, playing musical instruments)?
- Profession: What skills do you use in your work? What skills have you accumulated in previous jobs?
- Strengths: Aspects of yourself that you value inside and outside work.
- Qualities: What personal qualities do you possess? Eg kindness, stability, organization, patience, etc. Are you a good mother? brother? father? sister? daughter? son? friend? List all positive personal qualities.
- Vision: What is the vision that has got you to where you are now? We shall revisit vision in Chapter 14, but start to think about what your vision of life is. What do you stand for? What do you want to bring in to your life?
- Highlights: What memorable events can you think of that stand out in your life?

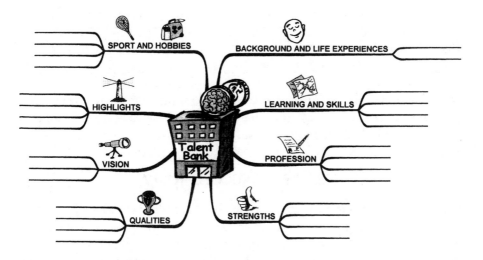

Figure 7.1 *The talent bank*

- Sports and hobbies: What sports and hobbies do you do? Whatever your capabilities, list down any you are involved in.

As well as work skills and personal qualities, remember your experiences at school or university, all of which can give you useful springboards on which to develop later in life.

2. Think about *transferable skills*. Exploring these helps you to see that you have choices about where you work. If you should become unhappy in your work or lose your job for some reason, it is good to know that there are many, many different things you can do in life to earn money. For example, if you like to travel you can become a tour guide; if you swim you can become a lifeguard; if you cook you can become a caterer; if you drive you can run a taxi company, and so on. Look over your talent bank and add below as many different careers as you can think of when you look at your skills, qualities and experiences.

_____

_____

_____

3. Now that you have had an opportunity to review your talents and successes, what conclusions can you draw? Look at your present working life and how you have created it. Consider how you can use this success to breed more success. Write your ideas below.

_____

_____

_____

Reflecting on your past successes can help to understand why you excel at certain subjects and topics more than others, so look back over your life so far as you complete the next exercise.

EXERCISE 7.2 SUCCESS REVIEW

Think about subjects and activities you excel at or find easy to achieve or to learn. List them below. Then think about subjects you find difficult and list them. Then, for each, analyse and consider why you excel at one subject and why you find another subject more difficult. Is it the subject area itself? Do you prefer broad picture and more conceptual subjects such as English, history or philosophy, or detailed and analytical subjects, such as the sciences? Does the environment affect your performance? Or the people you have to interact with? See if you can find connecting links that help you to identify your preferences. Once you have done so, it is easier to create those features in your life in the future.

Good subjects/activities   Why I find this subject easy

_____

_____

_____

_____

_____

Difficult subjects/activities   Why I find this subject difficult

_____

_____

_____

_____

_____

How can you use these insights in the future?

I realize that I find subjects and activities with the following ingredients easiest and most fulfilling because:

_____

_____

_____

I shall play to my strengths by:

_____

_____

_____

CELEBRATE

Success is a moving target. To have reached the position you are now in, you will already have achieved some of your targets along the way. It is important to stop and appreciate successful moments. Success gives you learning points, in the same way as do mistakes. In both cases it is easy to steam ahead onto the next challenge without giving sufficient time to reflect on how you have achieved your successes. Success can even breed failure if you allow yourself to become complacent or do not review the situation sufficiently to learn how you achieved it.

Once you and your team achieve a goal, do you take time to savour the moment of success or are you off and running on to the next goal?

EXERCISE 7.3 MY SUCCESS SCRAPBOOK

As your brain stores information in pictures and images it is important to recall these successful pictures from your past. We cannot emphasize enough how powerful this exercise is. Go back through all your records, files, and ask your relatives and friends to do the same, collecting all the pictures, press cuttings, articles, awards, etc you can find that cover your previous successes in life.

Next purchase a sturdy scrapbook. Then assemble in chronological order a history of your successes to date. Go back as far as you can, to school days, boy scouts or girl guides, the earlier the better. You will be surprised by what you can dig up. Spend time creating this chronological history of success. When it is complete, spend time frequently reviewing and updating it. Think and talk about each page or each event.

Each time you go back and relive your scrapbook you strengthen your success-recall process. The process reminds you that you have the power to achieve goals that you may well have forgotten about. Continue to build this up and add any new successful events.

Each small success has its own quality. To learn from your successes you need to be able to stop and consider how you achieved it. If a project has gone well at work, investigate your methods in case there is a useful formula that you could use on another project. Think also of other people within your organization who could benefit from your case study of success. And then celebrate!

EXERCISE 7.4 CELEBRATION

Make a list of how you would like to celebrate the achievement of your goals (for example, going out for a celebratory meal; drinking champagne; going to the theatre; taking time to stop and read a book you have been meaning to read).

_____

_____

_____

Are you able to share your success without feeling embarrassed about your achievements? It is interesting to watch football stars hugging and kissing each other in front of thousands of screaming fans after scoring a goal. These highly paid and highly trained athletes realize how important it is to acknowledge their successes and share that excitement with their fans. Enthusiasm being contagious, you may well have felt the thrill of your favourite team scoring victories.

What is your response and reaction when you have victories and what is the response of your peers and support team, be they work colleagues, family, friends or mentors? We often get feedback from people in business that there is more recognition of things that go wrong than recognition of success. If this is the culture in your organization, it can lead to resentment.

It also gives the brains in your company more negative than positive messages.

Many people get blocked from moving forward to make positive changes by focusing on the occasions when something went wrong previously, rather than when something went right. Therefore, in going into a meeting with a colleague with whom they have been in conflict, they focus on situations where communication went wrong: 'Oh dear, I have to go and see Gerry and he and I just don't see eye to eye.'

THE SUCCESS-RECALL PROCESS

Using successful moments as a springboard when facing new or difficult tasks at work can be more effective. For example, if you are about to meet a new client, or have to give a presentation or discuss a sensitive topic with a difficult colleague, you will have an increased ability to manage your emotions positively if you remind yourself what it feels like to feel good.

Focus on situations (even if quite separate) when things went right for you. The energy you create around you when things go well is infectious and you can use that energy to make a start on the right foot, instead of recreating old problems. Try this now in the next exercise.

EXERCISE 7.5 SUCCESS-RECALL PROCESS

1. Take five minutes to think back to a time in your life where you accomplished something you were proud of. First build up the pictures through the prompt questions below, then close your eyes and relive it. Think of the event and picture it in your mind's eye. Make it colourful. Be in it, as if you were there now.

Where were you?

_____

_____

_____

Who was with you?

_____

_____

_____

What were people saying? Can you hear people talking to you in their own voices?

_____

_____

_____

Was someone shaking your hand?

_____

_____

_____

Conjure up the emotion. How did it feel?

_____

_____

_____

What did you say to other people?

_____

_____

_____

What were you saying to yourself?

_____

_____

_____

How were you standing? Imagine it as if you were there now and adopt the physiology.

_____

_____

_____

How were you breathing, eg shallowly or deeply?

_____

_____

_____

2. Now you have identified the ingredients of the experience, take a moment or two to close your eyes and relive that event as if it were happening today. Conjure up the feelings, pictures and sounds. Think of a word that will remind you of it. You will be able to use this word as a trigger to remind you of this success experience.

Trigger Word:

_____

_____

_____

If this above exercise was a new experience for you, remember that the event was something which you have stored away in your memory and have access to at any time. Each time you go back and relive it, you strengthen this success-recall process. In the next exercise you will discover how to use it to help you achieve a goal.

Sports psychologists use this technique to train winning teams. You may have noticed athletes pause and close their eyes before an event. What they are doing is exactly what you have done: to go back and relive a success which then changes their present physiological and emotional state to one of successful anticipation. Smart business people and teams are beginning to use the same techniques themselves. Major organizations such as the Chase Manhattan Bank are now using sports psychologists to coach their teams in success.

Consider what you have learnt from this exercise and plan some occasions when you can use it in the future to empower yourself, for example before giving a speech, preparing for a difficult meeting, giving a client some bad news. You might want to connect this success memory with a physical object that you carry around with you daily, eg on a key chain or a ring or your watch, so that every time you handle or look at it you are reminded of your successful event. Without this review, it is very easy to forget that you have this particular technique at your fingertips.

In the next exercise you use the success-recall process to help you to manage a difficult situation you have coming up in the future.

EXERCISE 7.6 THE UPLIFT OSCARS

Think of a difficult or challenging situation you are likely to have in the near future:

_____

_____

_____

Think how you would like to feel: calm? confident? articulate? strong?

_____

_____

_____

Spend a couple of minutes and take yourself back to a situation when you experienced a similar feeling to the one you would like to feel (as we did in

Figure 7.2 *The Uplift Oscars*

the previous exercise). It does not matter where you were at the time. What you need to create is the physical and emotional state, which is not necessarily dependent on the event involved.

Now, as well as recreating that experience within you as you did in Exercise 7.5, imagine and visualize yourself feeling like that in the future event. In your mind's eye, see yourself handling the situation in the way you would like to do so.

Start to see yourself as if it were a movie and you were seated in a cinema watching yourself, the star, acting out the scene. Then step into the movie and become the hero or heroine. Run the movie in your head as many times as you wish, until you are comfortable with it and the outcome. You can change the dialogue, the outcome, anything you wish. Add a musical score if you like. You are both star and director: it is your movie. This technique of rehearsing a future activity sets your brain up for success and is extremely powerful.

Comment on your experiences:

This 'uplift' technique can work as well for a presentation or meeting as it can for simply getting out of bed on a Monday morning knowing that you have a difficult week ahead. Focus on your positive experiences. Feel strong and enthusiastic in each moment. These techniques can radically improve the everyday quality of your life as you integrate them into your conscious mind on a daily basis.

The information that you have gathered about yourself and your life so far can act as an anchor in any storm. Keep adding to your talent bank as you continue through your business life. Notice your transferable skills. Capture words of appreciation and praise from work colleagues and clients. Write these down for future reference. In the ebb and flow of life they can bolster you and help you to go forward in new directions.

When you know your strengths, you experience a greater sense of security and self-confidence. Whatever challenges you may experience, you can tap into your inner resources and know that you have, within your own success story, the capability to withstand setbacks and create positive results.

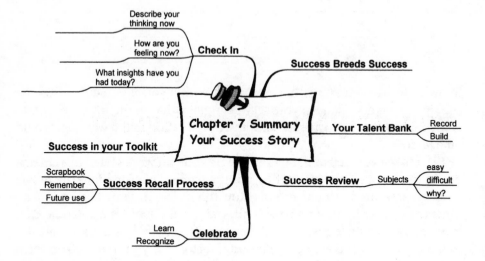

Figure 7.3 *Summary: your success story*

8

You Are Multi-Intelligent

In many Western cultures there is a tendency to place a good deal of emphasis on academic qualifications and not enough on the richness and variety of skills and talents of the sort we have begun to highlight in the previous chapter. The over-emphasis on academic results originated in the past, when the route to the boardroom often lay through the particular school or university that you had attended. Certificates of one sort or another were what companies sought out and recognized for recruitment and promotion. It was thought, until recently, that we had only two major intelligences – mathematical/logical and linguistic.

Things have changed. The Confederation of British Industry issued a report in April 1998 recommending that schools include personal development as an essential ingredient for preparing children for their careers. This was supported in a business survey taken in the UK in May 1999 by PricewaterhouseCoopers, which demonstrated that organizations are now looking for 'creativity, communication and adaptability'. Whilst knowledge and skills are still required, the following trends were listed as the most likely changes in the organization of the future:

- more individual accountability and responsibility (68 per cent);
- more flexible working (60 per cent);
- fewer, more skilled staff (42 per cent);

- more part-time staff (40 per cent); and
- more older staff (20 per cent).

If this is the case, people need to develop the ability to adapt and be flexible and, to continue to learn, they need to understand more about how they learn best. They also need to be able to shift their focus from the strictly skill-based qualifications to the more intangible skills of self-motivation, discipline, time management, communication and the development of the inner confidence required to manage change.

Our experience of consulting for companies throughout different sectors of industry across the globe indicates there is an underlying inclination to believe we are not as smart as we really are. This naturally varies depending on the culture in which you live. For example, in the UK the aversion to being a 'show-off' is instilled from an early age. If people do well they will often placate their peer group by saying something like 'well it was just a fluke' rather than accept that they achieved a goal through their own very real abilities.

This is not necessarily the case in other countries. For example, in the United States, parts of Europe or African countries, people are generally encouraged to promote their success. However, despite these regional cultural differences, lack of self-esteem is still a major problem, whether you are at the top or the bottom of an organization.

We meet many senior executives who experience anxiety that they have got to the top of their career but may not have as many academic or professional qualifications as some of those who work under them. This can develop into a fear of being 'found out' for not being as 'clever' as their position denotes.

Of course, the truth is that they have used different forms of intelligence to attain their goals and that academic qualifications are not in themselves necessarily of practical application in the workplace. It also has to be remembered that university education, for example, was not as readily available in the period when many of the senior managers of today were starting out on their careers.

Indeed, there are many examples of people who have achieved great success in business despite having left school without completing further education – Richard Branson of Virgin and Bill Gates of Microsoft, to mention just two. Einstein and Edison are examples from previous generations.

This demonstrates that the multi-faceted nature of the human being makes us much smarter than any paper 'diploma' can denote. The breakthrough in this area is the work of Professor Howard Gardner of Harvard, who advanced a theory of multiple intelligences that we use constantly throughout the day. Therefore we are not just using logic and linguistic intelligence but also musical, interpersonal, intrapersonal, spatial and kinaesthetic intelligence.

This breakthrough in thinking is hard for many people to accept, especially those brought up in an educational system which placed a tremendous emphasis on intelligence tests based, as we mentioned earlier, on only two of the intelligences: logical/mathematical and linguistic.

Here is a brief review of the seven intelligences identified by Gardner.

1. *Linguistic intelligence* is the core operations of language, our ability to use words.
2. *Logical-mathematical intelligence* refers to the ability to play with and to manipulate the 'numerical alphabet' as well as exhibiting competence in logical thought. This intelligence includes appreciating abstract relationships.
3. *Musical intelligence* enables people to exhibit a good sense of rhythm. This intelligence can also include the ability to listen carefully to the subtleties of the tone of voice.
4. *Visual/spatial intelligence* is the ability to perceive the world in three or more dimensions, resulting in competence to work with inter-relationships of networks and systems.
5. *Bodily kinaesthetic intelligence* is the ability to engage competently in sports, dancing, work and any area where physical mobility is necessary. Your physical stance is important in the message it sends to business associates and clients.
6. *Intrapersonal intelligence* is the ability to understand oneself and make beneficial progress based on this knowledge. The emphasis of this book is on intrapersonal knowledge. Your ability to be able to navigate according to a good, clear, mental model or map that represents you at any point in time directly affects the unfolding of your life.
7. *Interpersonal intelligence* is the intelligence of communicating with others, enjoying the company of other people both at work and socially. This is a very crucial intelligence in today's world, especially where you are working with teams.

Professor Gardner is continually updating his research into multiple intelligence. We have also identified five related areas of intelligence as a result of our research with business executives around the world.

8. *Intuitive intelligence* is sensory knowledge which enables you to tap into the intuitive part of your brain and sense the unseen and the

unspoken, coming to decisions based upon internal feelings rather than logical analytical intelligence.

9. *Technical intelligence* is the ability successfully to use technology and to update skills to manage the ever-expanding technology that becomes available daily.

10. *Creative intelligence* is the ability to come up with new ideas, concepts and solutions. It is a very important leadership characteristic, where vision and immediate creative breakthroughs are required on a daily basis.

11. *Financial intelligence* is the ability to know how to manage the flow of assets and to create wealth.

12. *Philosophical intelligence* is the ability to bring wisdom into the workplace and seek and find a sense of purpose in life.

The following exercise is designed to help you ascertain which of these intelligences you are using.

EXERCISE 8.1 MULTIPLE INTELLIGENCES

On Figure 8.1, mark on a scale of 0–10, with 0 being the lowest and 10 being the highest, your current assessment of each respective intelligence.

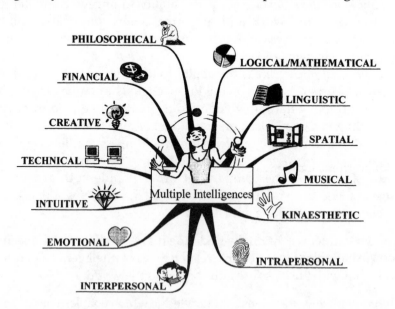

Figure 8.1 *Your multiple intelligence*

EXERCISE 8.2 DESCRIBE YOUR INTELLIGENCE

Now that you are aware of the different types of intelligence and your overview assessment, take a moment to think about how you use these intelligences in your daily business life and write in or draw the examples in the spaces provided below:

Linguistic intelligence

Logical-mathematical intelligence

Musical intelligence

Visual/spatial intelligence

Bodily kinaesthetic intelligence

Intrapersonal intelligence

Interpersonal intelligence

Intuitive intelligence

Technical intelligence

Creative intelligence

Financial intelligence

Philosophical intelligence

Emotional intelligence

You are strongly recommended to develop all of the above intelligences as you will find they have a synergistic effect, ie strengthening one strengthens them all. To remain effective in today's workplace, it is advisable to become aware of how you learn and to develop your ability to keep learning new and diverse skills and information.

Here are some tips on how to develop each individual intelligence.

1. *Linguistic*: You communicate with people through language. To maintain a powerful impression, it is important to monitor the words you use and to ensure that the message you are giving is clear and positive. As research has demonstrated that there is a direct correlation between income and vocabulary, you may like to read subject areas that you have not read before. This will expose you to new words and language.
2. *Logical*: Develop your ability to approach tasks in a logical way. Scrutinize your reports and presentations to ensure that there is a logical sequence. Prioritize your workload in a logical order.
3. *Musical*: You use your musical abilities every day at work through listening to the tone and pace of people's voices. Develop the musical tonality of your own voice and develop the ability to listen to the voices of those around you. Learn to play a musical instrument. This could be anything from an inexpensive recorder to an electronic keyboard. Sing some more in your shower and car.
4. *Visual-spatial*: You use your spatial intelligence at work in the way you design and lay out your working environment. Look at your office and question your spatial intelligence as you gauge whether the office layout supports your work. For example, if you want back-office staff to improve communication with front-office staff, are they within easy access of one another? The physical environment of your office can sabotage your policies unless you develop your spatial intelligence. Take up a hobby such as painting or drawing with either a good art teacher or a good art book to gain an understanding of perspective.
5. *Bodily-kinaesthetic*: Your physical conduct within the workplace is an important part of your image. The way you walk into a room or walk to the coffee machine says a great deal about you. Straighten your spine, open your shoulders and relax your neck. Develop a sense of who you are and the image you want to convey to people as you move around. Learn ballroom, salsa or tango dancing or develop any sport, individual or team, to gain strength and suppleness.
6. *Intrapersonal*: You are developing your intrapersonal intelligence as you read this book. You could also attend workshops, lectures or seminars

on the art of self-knowledge. Keep a daily diary of your observations about yourself. Writing about yourself in the third person can be insightful.

7. *Interpersonal*: Communication is a key leadership tool. Develop your understanding of yourself and others as you read this book. Join public-speaking classes, become active in your community, become aware of the part you play in social interaction.

8. *Intuitive*: It is helpful to be aware of unspoken messages at work. Think of some occasions when you could intuitively sense that a person's words did not tally with their body language. Start listening to the internal messages from your body: remember the feeling you had when the telephone rang and you knew who it was going to be.

9. *Technical*: Our ability to adapt successfully to change and keep learning can be dependent on our capacity to learn to keep abreast of technological change. Read books on how computers work. Take a course at a local college on a technical subject, eg technical drawing or computing. Study the instruction manuals for videocassette recorders, computers and fax machines.

10. *Creative*: Every company and every individual needs to maintain their competitive edge through continuing innovation. Creativity is not just for artists: it encompasses finding new ways to do things and developing new products or services. Read books on creativity, play creative games such as chess, think of new ways to do things. Do something different each day.

11. *Financial*: It is helpful to have a basic understanding of finance both in your business and in your personal life. Read a financial newspaper and a financial magazine weekly. Study stock markets and learn the language. Read about the lives of great financial geniuses.

12. *Philosophical*: More and more people are seeking a purpose in their work and wanting to find meaning in their life. It can help to read the great masters of philosophy available in paperback from your local bookstore or library. Think how you would apply their principles to your daily business situations: what are we here for? How does your work fit into your philosophical and value systems?

EXERCISE 8.3 DEVELOPING MY MULTI-INTELLIGENCES

List below an action plan based on three types of intelligence you wish to develop first and what actions you intend to take to develop them:

1. Intelligence

_____

_____

_____

Actions to be taken to develop this intelligence

_____

_____

_____

_____

_____

_____

2. Intelligence

_____

_____

_____

Actions to be taken to develop this intelligence

_____

_____

_____

_____

_____

_____

3. Intelligence

_____

_____

_____

Actions to be taken to develop this intelligence

_____

_____

_____

_____

_____

_____

Developing your intelligences gives you broader perspective. Much of our academic and professional life is geared towards an area of expertise or specialization. However, this can narrow your thinking and limit your perspective. The urgent pressures of deadlines and the culture of long working hours, lunch at the desk, etc does not allow for time to have general broad-scope discussions with people in other departments or other industries.

There is a balance to be striven for whereby it is possible to be an expert in one's field and yet remain a generalist. The decisions you make in business demand this balance. If you narrow your focus too much you cannot see the broad picture or the longer term world trends. Your decisions are then based on only a small platform of information.

Developing your multiple intelligences helps you to discover links, connections and associations, which strengthens understanding and results in you becoming a far more broadly intelligent and effective business executive. You will notice that your horizons will expand as well as your interests and knowledge about the world around you. This will open you up to new opportunities you may not have seen before.

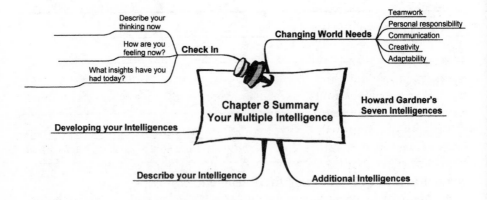

Figure 8.2 *Summary: your multiple intelligence*

9

The Pressure Pot

Every year life at work is becoming increasingly complicated. Little has prepared you for this age of deadlines, technological advances and ever-increasing expectations of performance. The business environment, where downsizing, loss of jobs, and multi-skilling are commonplace, compounds this problem. People of all ages find themselves being made redundant. This leaves many skilled and talented people unemployed while those still in employment are doing twice the workload and living in fear of losing their own jobs at some future time.

This culture of fear predominates in many organizations and can adversely affect people's ability to take decisions that may involve risk or the necessity to use initiative. It can also destroy loyalty to the company, and trust. Fear inevitably limits creativity and innovation, as well as preventing honest and open communication.

Stressful situations will always exist in our lives and a degree of stress can be beneficial in motivating you to achieve your goals and to perform at your best. This chapter will help you gain a balance that enables you to enjoy the challenges rather than feel fearful of them.

To maintain peak performance and the ability to manage change, it is advisable to learn how to manage your own stress. We suggest a simple process that will help you to manage stress:

1. Identify the situations and people that are causing you stress.
2. Notice any physical symptoms you may be experiencing.
3. Become aware of the behavioural symptoms of stress in yourself and in your colleagues.
4. Take charge of the situation through the Three Changes Process you learnt in Chapter 4:
   - Change your Thinking;
   - Change your Physiology;
   - Change the Circumstances.

STRESSFUL INFLUENCES

Begin by identifying some of the situations and people that cause you stress. As a means to greater awareness of the problem areas of your life, it can be helpful to record these on Figure 9.1. This figure is a visual method of studying, clarifying, simplifying and grading the sources of stress in your life. It enables you to focus objectively on the circumstances around

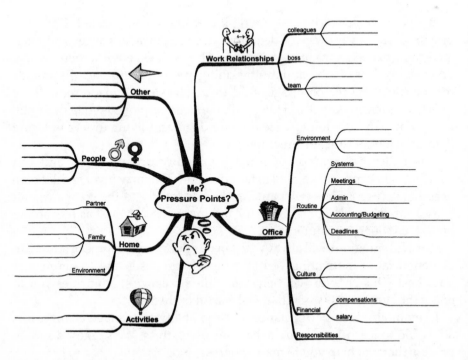

Figure 9.1 *Your pressure points*

you and investigate the factors that influence your daily activities. Consider both work and domestic situations, as each will be having an impact on the other.

In a work situation you may be experiencing stress from colleagues, bosses or subordinates. You may also find the structure and culture of your organization difficult to manage. Role ambiguity can cause stress, as can work overload or, indeed, being underworked. Changes at work – new job, new bosses, mergers, new recruits, new systems – can be measured and graded to identify problem areas.

Each item marked is given a grade of stress: 0 is low stress, 10 is high stress. You are also asked to consider and grade how much stress you may cause others. Once the problem areas become clear to you, it is easier for you to create a strategy to manage them.

EXERCISE 9.1 PRESSURE POINTS

1. Put yourself in the centre of Figure 9.1 and identify any causes of stress you may be experiencing. Put the major problem areas closest to the centre. These can include people, situations, culture, challenges, self-activated problems, etc.

2. Having identified some of the major areas of stress in your life, answer the following questions.

What is your definition of stress?

_____

_____

_____

In what ways does stress benefit your life?

_____

_____

_____

Are there any common patterns in what causes you stress?

_____

_____

_____

What stress might you be causing others?

_____

_____

_____

What might you wish to change?

_____

_____

_____

What is one thing you could immediately do to alleviate some of the stress you have identified in the map?

_____

_____

_____

THE CHEMISTRY OF STRESS

Your response to stress will have physical repercussions in your body. This is what people refer to as 'the mind–body connection'. We discussed the chemistry of thinking earlier. As we have been demonstrating throughout this book, your thinking sets up a chemical response in your brain. This then ripples through your body; negative thinking, or stress, sets up its own series of physical reactions in what is commonly known as the 'fight or flight' response. Every thought you have changes your chemistry.

Your thinking determines whether or not you experience stress. You cannot always change the situations you face every day but you can change your responses to them. Thinking is one area in which you can take control of your life. Allowing yourself to dwell on negative thoughts generates the stress response in your body and a long-term chemical stress reaction can harm your health.

If something happens to you that you perceive to be stressful, a neural message is received into the brain through the five senses and a physical response takes place in the body. For example, you are standing on a platform of a railway station waiting for a train to take you to an important meeting. You hear an announcement that the train has been cancelled. This

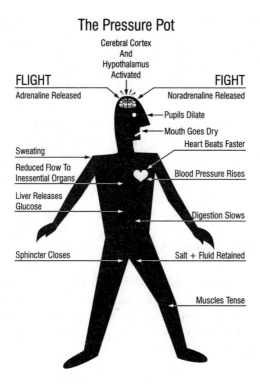

The Pressure Pot

Cerebral Cortex
And
Hypothalamus
Activated

FLIGHT

Adrenaline Released

FIGHT

Noradrenaline Released

Pupils Dilate

Mouth Goes Dry

Heart Beats Faster

Sweating

Reduced Flow To
Inessential Organs

Blood Pressure Rises

Liver Releases
Glucose

Digestion Slows

Sphincter Closes

Salt + Fluid Retained

Muscles Tense

Figure 9.2   *The pressure pot*

message is received through your auditory sense, transmitted to the brain and the degree of stress you experience will be determined by your own response to this news.

Depending on the situation, the neurons work on the sympathetic and parasympathetic nervous systems and produce either adrenaline, to give immediate energy for a 'flight' response, or noradrenaline, to release energy for a 'fight' response. Noradrenaline is therefore more likely to be produced in a situation where you feel there is an opportunity to be in control. In the example we give above, neither flight nor fight are necessarily appropriate responses to the information that a train has been cancelled.

Cortisol is also released into the body. In the short term this supports the body's physical responses but it has been demonstrated that during long-term stress cortisol may contribute to lowering the immune system and causing illness.

These flight or fight responses are designed to prepare the human body for a physical activity, and date back from the time of early man. This is a serious problem today for those in business, as much stress is caused by daily mental or emotional problems rather than by events that require a physical reaction. The experience on the railway station, a difficult telephone call, conflict with a colleague, or the prolonged fear of losing a job as a result of a merger or downsizing are today's equivalent to the caveman's mammoth.

During stress, the majority of the body's energy supplies are diverted to activate physical strength. Meanwhile, your upper thinking brain is deprived of the vital energy it needs for clarity of thought. The stress response thus supports immediate and spontaneous decision-making about survival but does not assist you in the complex problem-solving activities of the workplace. In addition, without physical release of the stress hormones through the fight or flight activities, the build-up of chemicals in the body has no opportunity to disperse and can cause long-term health problems.

Absenteeism as a result of stress-related illness is costing industry billions of pounds. It is therefore critical both for your health, your continuing high performance at work and your organization in general to keep stress levels low. With awareness and a proven set of skills, many of these problems can be both prevented and alleviated.

BECOMING AWARE OF YOUR OWN PHYSICAL SYMPTOMS OF STRESS

It is essential to tune into the warning signals your body gives you and to become aware of your own physical symptoms of stress. These signals tell you when you need to take action to relieve your stress.

Physical reactions to stress include increased heart rate and blood pressure as the blood is pumped towards the muscles. Hands and feet tend to become cold as the blood leaves the skin surface. You may sweat, which enables the body to be cooled during physical exertion. Breathing becomes faster, pupils dilate and the mouth becomes dry. Fatty acids are released into the blood and, as cholesterol is released, veins become constricted and there is the risk of the build-up of arterial blockages. Digestive problems are common symptoms of stress, in the form of constipation or diarrhoea. The glucose released by the liver gives short-term energy but can cause problems over time.

Therefore, with prolonged stress, the chances of serious illness are increased considerably. You may yourself know of people who have suffered heart attacks at work and others within your organization who are frequently ill with persistent minor ailments. If you notice persistent symptoms of illness and absenteeism in members of your team or other work colleagues, you might like to investigate whether these people are under pressure. It is possible that a simple change might alleviate their problems. A client recently told us of her surprise when, on visiting her doctor with a minor infection, he asked her whether she was stressed at work. She replied that she was, as there had been recent changes of personnel within her team. Increasingly, the medical profession is recognizing the connection between minor illness and stress.

When stress becomes overwhelming, or when people are not noticing their own physical and emotional symptoms, they can sometimes experience 'panic attacks'. During a panic attack a person feels breathless and may experience pain in their chest. This can be very frightening as people can confuse the symptoms with heart attacks. Should you experience a panic attack, it is always advisable to visit your doctor to ensure that there is not something physically wrong. If not, then have a set of affirmations readily available in your mind, such as 'I can manage this situation, this is a panic attack and I can think myself out of it'. These cognitive techniques have been proven to be effective. Should you experience any of the symptoms on a continuous basis, it is always advisable to consult your doctor.

As your health and the health of each member of an organization or team is of paramount importance, you may like to suggest to your colleagues and teams that they are watchful of danger signs both in themselves and in those around them.

EXERCISE 9.2 BE AWARE

Consider whether you have noticed any of the following stress symptoms in your own body:

- Blurred vision
- Bowel disorders
- Difficulty in swallowing
- Disturbed sleep patterns and insomnia
- Dizziness
- Dry mouth
- Faster breathing
- Faster heart rate
- Headaches

- High blood pressure
- Nausea or 'butterfly' stomach
- Nervous indigestion
- Palpitations
- Panic attacks
- Rashes and allergies
- Sexual difficulties
- Sweaty palms
- Tension in neck, back and shoulders
- Ulcers

BEHAVIOURAL SYMPTOMS OF STRESS

Alongside the physical symptoms of stress, you are likely to notice changes of behaviour in yourself or in work colleagues. These can be a particularly helpful indicator of stress in work colleagues.

EXERCISE 9.3 RECOGNIZING STRESS

1. Mark any behavioural symptoms you have noticed in yourself:

Early warning signals:

- Being too busy to talk
- Eating at desk, or skipping meals
- Drinking many cups of coffee
- Grumbling about work situations to colleagues
- Working long hours

'It's getting too much'

- Irritability and impatience
- Aggressive behaviour
- Becoming upset over minor problems, slamming drawers, etc
- Headaches and/or gastric symptoms
- Smoking or drinking more
- Insomnia
- Forgetfulness
- Disorganized desk or obsessive tidiness

'I need help'

- Inability to cope with workload
- Dizziness and depression
- Minor illness
- Palpitations
- Anxiety/panic attacks
- Lack of interest and attention
- Inability to perform simple tasks
- Anti-social behaviour
- Loss of energy
- Burn-out

Note in which area you have the most ticks. Note your comments:

_____

_____

_____

2. Have you noticed any of these symptoms in your colleagues? If so, who and when?

_____

_____

_____

Monitor your health and behaviour on a daily basis in future. Degrees of stress will always exist and can be beneficial to performance. Notice when it motivates you and when it paralyses you. Ask yourself what is appropriate and helpful and whether changing your thinking would help you to achieve a healthy balance.

TYPE A AND TYPE B BEHAVIOUR

The following questionnaire has been developed by Professor Cary Cooper of UMIST from the Bortner Type A profile. It will help you to assess your own behaviour tendencies.

EXERCISE 9.4 TYPE A BEHAVIOUR

In the table overleaf, circle one number for each of the statements which best reflects the way you behave in your everyday life. For example, if you

	1	2	3	4	5	6	7	8	9	10	11	
Casual about appointments	1	2	3	4	5	6	7	8	9	10	11	Never late
Not competitive	1	2	3	4	5	6	7	8	9	10	11	Very competitive
Good listener	1	2	3	4	5	6	7	8	9	10	11	Anticipates what others are going to say (nods, attempts to finish for them)
Never feels rushed (even under pressure)	1	2	3	4	5	6	7	8	9	10	11	Always rushed
Can wait patiently	1	2	3	4	5	6	7	8	9	10	11	Impatient while waiting
Takes things one at a time	1	2	3	4	5	6	7	8	9	10	11	Tries to do many things at once; thinks about what to do next
Slow deliberate talker	1	2	3	4	5	6	7	8	9	10	11	Emphatic in speech, fast and forceful
Cares about satisfying him/herself no matter what others may think	1	2	3	4	5	6	7	8	9	10	11	Wants good job recognized by others
Slow doing things	1	2	3	4	5	6	7	8	9	10	11	Fast (eating, walking)
Easy-going	1	2	3	4	5	6	7	8	9	10	11	Hard driving (pushing yourself and others)
Expresses feelings	1	2	3	4	5	6	7	8	9	10	11	Hides feelings
Many outside interests	1	2	3	4	5	6	7	8	9	10	11	Few interests outside work/home
Unambitious	1	2	3	4	5	6	7	8	9	10	11	Ambitious
Casual	1	2	3	4	5	6	7	8	9	10	11	Eager to get things done

Plot total score below:

Type B		Mid-point		Type A
14	$\longrightarrow$	84	$\longrightarrow$	154

Source: Cooper's adaptation of the Bortner Type A Scale, taken from Cary L Cooper, Rachel D Cooper and Lynn H Eaker, *Living with Stress*, Penguin, 1988, as adapted from RW Bortner, A Short Rating Scale as a Potential Measure of Pattern A Behaviour, (1969) *Journal of Chronic Diseases*, 22, pp 87–91.

are generally on time for appointments, for the first point you would circle a number between 7 and 11. If you are usually casual about appointments you would circle one of the lower numbers between 1 and 5.

Type A behaviour is commonly associated with people who are high achievers and place a great deal of importance on identifiable goals. They are very competitive and tend to lead life at a frenetic pace. They often carry out several activities at once – for instance while talking on the telephone they will at the same time be reading a report on their desk and planning a meeting. They experience guilt if they have time to relax. These tendencies make Type A people more prone to stress.

Type As do things quickly, including speech, movement and eating, and will hurry the speech of others by interrupting to finish a sentence. They will also tend to turn conversations towards their own interests. Indeed, they can tend to become obsessed with their own pursuits and become unaware of other aspects of life around them. They place importance on the value of time and how it is spent. Therefore, they are usually rushed but seldom late.

We were working with a manager of an international company last year who showed signs of being Type A. She said that she had decided she would only work seven hours a day and that if she were to achieve this she had no time to stop and talk to those around her. She would therefore stride purposely down corridors and avoid contact with work colleagues and team members. She confessed that she found their conversations 'trivial and not work-focused' and was not interested in them. She did not eat lunch or take breaks.

Her management peers were taken aback by her approach, pointing out that the major task of a manager is to manage people and be available to listen to problems. A colleague pointed out that he knew he would not have discovered that a problem existed within his team had he not made the effort to engage a team member in conversation. Although the conversation began on the subject of general weekend pursuits, the trust that developed between them inspired the team member to have the confidence to share a vital piece of information with him that he might otherwise have missed.

There is a correlation between high-status jobs and Type A behaviour. These people have been shown to run a higher risk of heart disease due to the continuous pressure they place on their nervous system. However, they can also demonstrate resilience by means of their drive and perception, especially where this drive is accompanied by enthusiasm.

Type A behaviour can be modified once a person has become aware of their tendencies and wishes to change.

Type B people tend to be more relaxed and speak and act in a slower manner. This has nothing to do with intelligence but is simply a natural or learned behavioural style. Those who are extremely low on the Type B scale may find it difficult to motivate themselves. There is therefore a balance to be derived from being somewhere in the middle of the scale.

STRESSFUL THINKING

As we have demonstrated in the Five-Step Thinking System, negative or irrational thinking can, in itself, be the source of your stress. A definition of stress used by the Centre for Stress Management in London is: 'Stress occurs when pressure exceeds a person's perceived ability to cope.'

You can cause yourself stress by imagining something terrible will happen even though it has not actually happened. You can focus on the negative aspects of a situation and perceive that you cannot manage it, even though, if you took one step at a time, you might find you could manage it better than you had imagined. There may be some stressful factors in your life that you cannot change immediately (eg, a distracting open-plan environment) but you could learn to accept it by changing your attitude towards it.

Use the ABCDE model (see page 53 above) on a continuous basis to dispute your thinking:

A   What is happening?
B   What am I thinking?
C   What am I feeling?
D   Is my thinking logical? How might someone else respond? Is it helpful?
E   How else might I think?

Whenever you notice yourself feeling stressed, check into your thinking and ask yourself if you could look at the situation differently. Simple changes like 'yes, I do feel stressed but I can manage my feelings' will help to calm your immediate anxiety. It has been demonstrated that changing your thinking changes your physiology and allows the negative effects of stress to dissolve.

STILLING THE MIND

There is growing acceptance that it is beneficial to stop and still the mind. The practice of meditation is spreading in the Western world as a therapeutic method to counteract obsessive thinking.

In the United States, Dean Ornish, MD, has a growing following for his method of stress relief and reducing heart disease. Ornish, who has undertaken study after study, has a proven four-method approach for the ingredients of healthy living:

1. diet;
2. exercise;
3. meditation;
4. a loving, supportive environment.

It is interesting to note that many US medical insurance companies are now supporting Dr Ornish's methodology by reducing premiums for those on the programme.

Meditation is the ability to move from a beta brain frequency of 13–25 Hz (cycles per second) down to alpha, which is 8–12 Hz. It is in the alpha brainwave state that we experience daydreaming, fantasizing and visualization. It is also the state for relaxed alertness. Studies on accelerated learning have shown that individuals learn more effectively in this relaxed state than in the more common state of awakened tension that has previously been regarded as an appropriate state for learning. This state can be induced by relaxation exercises or by listening to the slow movements from baroque music.

Brain Waves

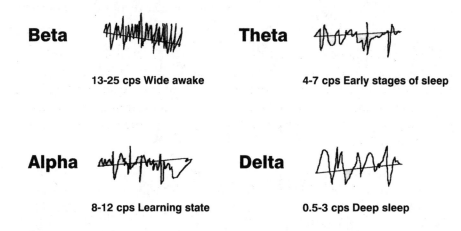

Beta — 13-25 cps Wide awake

Theta — 4-7 cps Early stages of sleep

Alpha — 8-12 cps Learning state

Delta — 0.5-3 cps Deep sleep

Figure 9.3 *Summary: brain waves*

The amount of mental activity that we experience every day in the work-place can be exhausting. Similarly, when we are in the midst of a crisis or working towards a deadline, we can experience momentary mental closedown when our system seems to be telling us that we can take no more pressure. If you experience such a feeling, it can be helpful to take a minute or two in which to allow your mind to focus on something peaceful or beautiful. This can refresh your whole mental, emotional and physical system. Listed below are two suggested methods you might care to try.

EXERCISE 9.5 MEDITATION

Meditation can be performed at any time during the day depending on your circumstances. You can choose to take 3 minutes or 30 minutes to still your mind.

Find a place where you can be quiet and uninterrupted. After taking a few deep, relaxing breaths, simply close your eyes to cut out distractions and concentrate on a sound or the sound of your breathing, or a word that could be repeated. By doing this you calm your mind, bringing it down from the active beta state to the alpha state. Turn your attention also to relaxing your body physically as your breathing becomes more rhythmic and calm. Gradually shift your focus from one area of your body to the next and relax the tension from neck, shoulders, back, fingers, jaw and scalp. Become aware of how you are feeling. Be mentally present in the moment.

Thoughts will come in and out of your mind. Just allow them to float like clouds in and out of your attention. Use the sound of your breathing to gently blow them away.

Most people find this refreshing. It lowers blood pressure and becomes easier with practice. As you progress with meditation you will find you will be able to do it any time and at any place, including crowded airports, on trains and buses.

EXERCISE 9.6 VISUALIZATION

An alternative way to meditate, and growing in popularity, is what is known as visualization. This process utilizes the right hemisphere mental skills of daydreaming and imagination. In a visualization, you either create the daydream yourself, listen to a tape or have someone read you the instructions.

Here is a suggested process. Place yourself into a comfortable position, normally with your back upright or lying on the floor, with your spine straight. Take three or four deep relaxing breaths and allow your body to relax. Release tension especially from your jaw, neck and shoulders.

Imagine yourself in a place or situation that uplifts and nurtures you. This can be factual or imagined, for example you may imagine yourself walking along a beach, walking through a meadow or in any other exotic or tranquil place you choose.

To strengthen the experience, use a multi-sensory approach by bringing into play as many of the senses as possible. For example, if you are walking along a beach, feel the sand against your feet and/or the sea water running over your toes. Smell the salt sea air, hear the seagulls and crashing waves. See sun-drenched beaches and taste the salt in your mouth.

If in a meadow, feel the grass under your feet, hear the birds in the trees and make the situation come alive. Allow yourself 5–20 minutes where your mind focuses on this pleasant experience. If other thoughts come into your mind, just let them drift away.

As you return to your normal conscious state, allow yourself to stretch, feel refreshed and come back into the present moment.

You need to practise this a few times to obtain the full benefits.

If you are a busy Type A person, an easy way to begin is to practise as you walk to work by focusing your attention on the sounds around you. How many sounds can you hear as you walk? Then become aware of how many physical feelings you are having – your feet on the pavement, your arms brushing against your sides, the feeling of your spine moving as you walk.

One of the major problems people discuss with us is 'lack of concentration'. This kind of mental-focus exercise will help you to develop your ability to focus more fully on what you are doing.

THINK YOUR WAY TO SELF-MANAGEMENT

Trying new ways of thinking, behaving and responding may feel awkward at first. If it does not feel awkward and a little uncomfortable, then it is unlikely that your approach is radically different from previous ways of behaving. Push yourself to apply new and untried methods so that you can build up the number of choices of behaviour that you have at hand. Put a visual trigger near your desk (a Post-It note or an uplifting poster) to remind you that you have a toolkit to help you manage stress in future.

TAKING CONTROL OF STRESS

With self-awareness and a set of mental and behavioural models, you can make immediate and beneficial changes to the way you handle stressful situations in the future. A greater understanding of stress enables you to have more control over your life. You will be able to choose your responses and be the controller and not the victim of your emotions. Learning how to manage your thinking, support your emotions, take control of your physiology and become aware that you do have choices regarding a change in your circumstances, can all help you to manage yourself.

The action plan that follows gives you the opportunity to use all the information you have gained so far. Take a situation that you have coming up in the near future and plan how you would like to manage it using the 'PEP Plan'.

EXERCISE 9.7 THE PROBLEM EMOTION PLAN (PEP)

Step One: State the problem

1. Clearly define a stressful problem or situation:

_____

_____

_____

2. Consider the consequences of continuing to have this problem:

_____

_____

_____

3. Consider the consequences of solving this problem:

_____

_____

_____

4. Is there any part of you that wants to maintain the problem? If so, why?

_____

_____

_____

Step Two: Identify the emotion

1. What emotion are you experiencing with this problem?

_____

_____

_____

2. When you think of the problem, identify a specific activating event (eg, if the problem stated in Step One is 'lack of self-confidence', note down a specific incident where you felt lacking in confidence):

_____

_____

_____

3. Belief/expectation/thoughts: write down any thoughts that were in your head at the time of the specific activating event. What were you thinking about? Were you putting pressurizing thoughts on yourself or on the others involved? (eg, 'I should be able to manage this situation', 'I can't handle this', or 'others must do what I want them to do'):

_____

_____

_____

4. Emotional consequence: think of the emotions you experienced. Are there any secondary emotions involved? (eg, feeling angry at being frightened):

_____

_____

_____

5. Disputing your thinking:

(a) Is your thinking logical? (eg, 'is it logical that I should feel stupid in this situation?' or 'whilst it is preferable that others do what I want them to do, is it logical to think that they must?'):

_____

_____

_____

(b) Would everyone in this situation respond the same way? How might others react?

_____

_____

_____

(c) Is your thinking supporting you and helping you achieve your goals? (eg, you want to achieve your targets but are thinking that you can't):

_____

_____

_____

Step Three: Develop your plan

1. What are your goals?

_____

_____

_____

2. In an ideal world, what do you really want to happen? Define your positive outcome:

_____

_____

_____

3. How many different ways are there to reach this goal?

_____

_____

_____

4. Prioritize one strategy to reach your goal ('I shall. . .'):

_____

_____

_____

5. In adopting this strategy how would you like to:
(a) Behave:

_____

_____

_____

(b) Feel emotionally:

_____

_____

_____

(c) Feel physically:

_____

_____

_____

6. What mental visual images would be helpful?

_____

_____

_____

7. What thoughts would be helpful?

_____

_____

_____

8. What interpersonal skills would be helpful?

_____

_____

_____

9. What biological interventions – or lack of interventions – would be helpful (eg, less caffeine, more deep breathing exercises)?

_____

_____

_____

10. Create a step-by-step Action Plan:

1st Step:

What?

_____

_____

_____

When?

_____

_____

_____

Why?

_____

_____

_____

2nd Step:

What?

_____

_____

_____

When?

_____

_____

_____

Why?

_____

_____

_____

You now have a greater understanding and awareness of how stress can turn you into a pressure pot about to explode! However, you also have a series of stress-reducing techniques to make sure that you remain confident and calm at all times. Take time to gain an understanding of how you can manage stress and not let stress manage you.

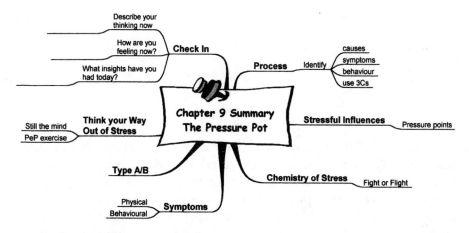

Figure 9.4 *Summary: 'the pressure pot'*

10

Working Relationships

All contact with other people occurs through communication. In today's fast-changing knowledge economy, communication has become the key management and leadership skill. The journey from business vision to the front-line worker takes place through communication. The achievement of set targets depends on each individual in that chain to make the journey successful. In the past, people would work alongside the same colleagues for many years. Nowadays people are changing roles and teams frequently. This demands an ability to build instant rapport, to understand others in the team as well as to stimulate creativity and innovation.

The ability to work together in groups develops the human and social capital of an organization. To manage your own career, you need to understand your present communication style and develop successful working relationships with a diverse group of clients and colleagues.

This interaction with others is probably the most challenging activity you will face and is closely linked with survival. Just as your ancestors would query whether someone was 'friend or foe', so in today's world this fundamental question still arises as part of your natural human response. In business you have many complex relationships with people and yet these basic survival instincts are still present.

There are numerous approaches to communication, teambuilding and relationship-management. Here are some that can be of practical help to you at work.

FIRST ENCOUNTERS

In the first five seconds of meeting with someone new, your brain and all your senses are computing information about this encounter. Tribal stereotyping and prejudice are unconsciously activated: does this person look different? Do they look threatening? Do you feel comfortable with their tone of voice? Can you understand the language they use? Have you come across this type of person before? What was your experience then? It is not surprising that it is often difficult to remember a person's name – your mind is focused on these more essential issues.

Inevitably, previous experiences and belief systems will shape your initial response to another person, and theirs to you. In fact, the linguistic content of what the person says to you represents only some 7 per cent of the information on which you base your view of them. The major message you receive, during face-to-face contact, comes from their body language: a startling 58 per cent of communication comes via the signals you pick up through the way they stand or gesture. The tone of voice used completes the picture.

The 'halo' effect of this first general impression is now well documented, demonstrating that these first few seconds can strongly influence whether you decide to accept or reject a person. These moments mark the success or failure of interviews, of sales presentations, of a first meeting with a new client or colleague, as well as many other interpersonal situations.

Consider how to make the most of yourself in those first moments, remembering that you are promoting your personal 'brand' in that short time. What messages might you want to communicate to people?

YOUR RELATIONSHIP WITH YOURSELF

It might be no surprise to you to learn that successful communication with others hinges to a great extent on successful communication with yourself. Simply the dialogue you experience from your 'inner voice' will either support or undermine you. You can only be to others what you are inside yourself.

Much of this inner dialogue stems from the relationship you had with your parents or other influential people in your life, and the relationship they had with each other. As we discussed in Chapter 2, 'Beliefs Drive Actions', you are likely, consciously or not, to have taken them as your role models and developed resulting patterns of behaviour.

Reflect how these influential people related to one another and what advantages or disadvantages this might have given you in the next exercise.

EXERCISE 10.1 ROLE MODELS OF COMMUNICATION

1. List who has influenced your communication style:

_____

_____

_____

_____

_____

_____

2. Were the above influences constructive and mutually rewarding? If so, why?

_____

_____

_____

_____

_____

_____

3. List the advantages of your role models' behaviour:

_____

_____

_____

_____

_____

4. List the disadvantages of your role models' behaviour:

_____

_____

_____

_____

_____

_____

STEREOTYPING

Your expectations of yourself and other people often come from the stereo-typing you were brought up with or have experienced as an adult. For example, you may 'expect' an artist or creative person to dress and communicate differently from a banker or accountant. These expectations can shape your communication with them and also, therefore, shape your communication with yourself ('self-talk'). If you have chosen banking as a profession, you may expect yourself to behave and communicate in the way you perceive a banker 'should' behave and communicate. You will have similar expectations of those around you.

Have you adapted your natural behaviour to what you consider to be appropriate to your work environment? This next exercise allows you to examine your communications within your chosen career.

EXERCISE 10.2 COMMUNICATION GAUGE

1. Quickly list below five or more sentences regarding how you 'should' or 'must' communicate at work (eg, 'I must not argue with superiors'):

_____

_____

_____

_____

_____

_____

2. Quickly list below five or more sentences regarding how others 'should' or 'must' communicate at work (eg, 'Others should treat me with consideration'):

_____

_____

_____

_____

_____

_____

3. Quickly list below how this thinking might be affecting your relationship with your colleagues or clients (eg, 'Clients believe I am professional' or 'My demands on my junior colleagues are causing friction'):

_____

_____

_____

_____

_____

4. Are your expectations rational or are they based upon personal perceptions? Can you think of more helpful ways of thinking about the expectations you have of those people with whom you communicate?

_____

_____

_____

_____

_____

In discovering your expectations, you are now able to decide whether they are helping you to build good working relationships with those around you or not.

PERFECTIONIST EXPECTATIONS IN COMMUNICATION

We wrote earlier (Chapter 3, 'Thinking about Thinking') of perfectionists and the stress that they can cause to those around them through unrealistically high expectations of themselves and other people. Perfectionists tend to think that there is a 'right and perfect' way of behaving and communicating. This is defined by their own personal standards and generally shaped by the culture in which they live and work. It can lead to critical and judgmental views of those who do not operate by these standards. This can be picked up and lead to defensive behaviour in others.

Being aware that your expectations are subjective helps you to decide whether your views are rational and helpful. You are now taking responsibility for your own responses and realizing that you can change your thinking. If someone does not behave the way you would expect, you could learn to think: 'I would prefer it if they behaved my way, but I can manage if they don't.'

Of course you can continue to hold certain personal opinions about behaviour and manners and yet remain objective, allowing others to be who they are. This is important in today's multi-cultural world.

Your expectations shape communication both with yourself and with other people. Questioning perfectionism allows you to see that everyone is fallible and life is seldom black and white. Flexibility towards other people's differences can allow you more readily to accept their unique contribution and help you to realize that you also are not perfect! This next exercise will give you some further insights.

EXERCISE 10.3 RELATIONSHIP REVIEW

Rate your effectiveness in developing and managing business relationships with:

	Weak	Needs developing	Acceptable	Good	Excellent
Superiors	1	2	3	4	5
Customers	1	2	3	4	5
Direct reports	1	2	3	4	5
Same sex	1	2	3	4	5
Opposite sex	1	2	3	4	5
Diversity	1	2	3	4	5

Add up your total. If you have scored 24 or more, this indicates that you have good understanding of how to manage yourself. If you have scored less than 18, consider whether you feel confident of yourself and are open to other people's viewpoints.

To develop more objective viewpoints of working relationships, use Exercise 10.4 to step mentally out of a recent situation and consider what other people might have been thinking.

STEPPING OUT

Changing behaviour means taking a few risks, but if a work relationship is not going as smoothly as you think it could, then it will mean stepping out of your old shoes and into some new ones and trying some different approaches. At first it can feel a little like acting, as the old behaviour can often seem more comfortable. So take one or two of the situations you recently experienced where communication may have been difficult.

EXERCISE 10.4 'NEW SHOES' THINKING

1. When could you use some of the following thoughts in communicating with yourself?
'Why don't you try?'

_____

_____

_____

'There are many ways of looking at something.'

_____

_____

_____

'What do you think?'

_____

_____

_____

2. When could you use some of the following thoughts in communicating with others?

'What can I do to help and support you?'

_____

_____

_____

'I would prefer it if. . .'

_____

_____

_____

'Have a go if you would like to. . .'

_____

_____

_____

'What do I really want here?'

_____

_____

_____

'Is there more of my natural self that I can show people at work?'

_____

_____

_____

3. How might this approach benefit your present working relationships?

_____

_____

_____

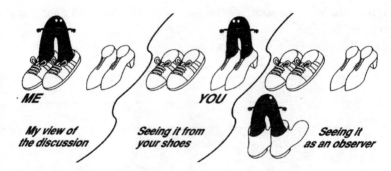

Figure 10.1 *'New shoes' thinking*

A POSITIVE END RESULT

A fast and effective way to improve relationships is to define what, in each specific instance, would be a win–win solution for you and the other party. People sometimes query the concept of win–win in business. In our experience, when people go for a win–win end-result, they are laying the foundations for a long-term relationship. For example, if you were to do a deal where you know you have got the upper hand in a financial negotiation with a client, it can feel as if you have 'won', or scored a point. However, if that client feels disadvantaged as a result of this negotiation, they may not wish to do business with you in the future. Imagine how you might feel, or have felt, were this to happen to you.

The first step in any encounter or meeting is to consider: 'What would be a positive end result for both of us?' There may need to be some compromise along the way, but without defining what, in your terms, is a positive end result it is easy to lose sight of your own needs or, indeed, to try to impose your needs upon the other person. This is particularly true if you are feeling emotional.

Your brain is a success-seeking mechanism, striving to reach the goals you set it and working 24 hours a day to achieve them. Without formulating your goals, you are likely to get stuck in the everyday problems that arise. Whenever you have a problem situation, the first thing to consider is what you would really like to happen, even if it does not feel immediately achievable.

EXERCISE 10.5 POSITIVE TARGETS

1. List below two of the communication situations you have recently experienced:

Figure 10.2 *Positive targets*

_____

_____

_____

_____

_____

_____

2. Write a positive end-result for yourself and the other people involved:

_____

_____

_____

_____

_____

_____

Your intention to work towards a positive outcome for all those involved will be reflected in your energy and your body language. Emotions are infectious and people notice them immediately. If someone walks into a meeting in a bad temper, everyone at that meeting is changed by that experience. If you walk into a meeting with negative thoughts and expectations of the people involved, or the outcome, that negativity will be radiating out to other people in the room. Focus on positive expectations and your positive end-result.

This chapter helped you discover your own expectations and responses to working relationships. You applied some models and methods which questioned whether your responses are reasonable and constructive and how they may be impacting those around you. Maintaining harmonious relationships with as many people as possible builds up an effective network of contacts. This network becomes your support in times of change. By defining a continuing positive outcome for each relationship, you build long-lasting and rich connections. In the next chapter, we discuss how to get value from a team or group of people with different styles of communicating.

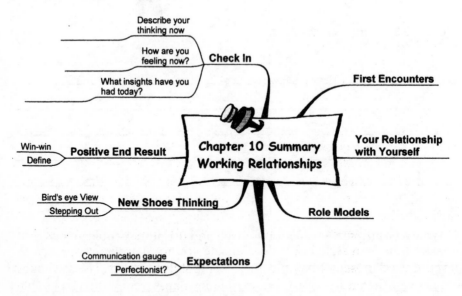

Figure 10.3   *Summary: working relationships*

11

Getting Value From Diversity

When working with people from different cultures and nationalities, you need to understand your own unique style and contribution and learn to value the unique contribution of others, even if you find their way of communicating confusing and even alien to you. It is often those whose way of thinking and communicating is most unlike your own who can take your own ideas to higher and more creative levels. Learning to appreciate this can, however, be challenging!

Various personality profiles have been developed that enable you to become aware of your own style and also become sensitive to the communication style of others. Through this awareness and understanding you can moderate and shape your language to clarify your message and make it easier for the other person to understand. This does not mean that you forsake your own style but it does enable you to plan your approach to meetings and presentations and adapt to the style of others. This facilitates a positive reaction to your recommendations and troubleshoots possible misunderstandings.

Some of these profiles measure personality and others measure different performance factors. We are including just two of the many profiles available: DiSC (Dominance, Influence, Stability and Compliance), which measures personality, and the HBDI (Herrmann Brain Dominance Instrument), which measures thinking preferences.

DiSC

In 1918, the Professor of Psychology at Columbia University, William Moulton Marsden, was asked by the military: 'Why is it that, despite identical training regimes, intakes of recruits behave differently?' Marsden spent ten years researching the subject and in 1928 published his book, *The Emotions of Normal People*, in which he posited that it is possible to predict human behaviour, *in given circumstances*.

The book was ignored in his lifetime, but in the 1950s another psychologist, William Cleaver, chanced upon the work, and, after much checking and experimentation, concluded that Marsden was right. He developed from it one of the most powerful methods available of assessing behaviour by measuring people's personality. More easily understood than Jung's ideas, but at least as effective, it put the use of psychometric management tools within the reach of the properly trained lay manager.

It is based upon two behavioural axes to measure responses to a self-reporting questionnaire. One is the aggressive–submissive axis, the other is the extrovert–introvert axis. We all sit somewhere on both these axes and the method provides us with four measurable characteristics called Dominance, Influence, Stability and Compliance (usually abbreviated to DiSC). Each of us has these four characteristics in our make-up in greater or lesser measure. However, one of them is always stronger than the others and is called the 'primary drive'.

EXERCISE 11.1 PERSONALITY STYLES

Read through the descriptions below and identify those elements that you believe reflect your own style.

Dominance

Someone whose primary drive is dominance is forceful and driving, demanding and impatient, and tends to be a director of people (ie, they tell, they do not ask). Such a person has an innate need to achieve, to overcome obstacles and problems. Consequently, their major motivations are winning and gaining power and control over their own future and their environment. They care not that you like them but demand respect for their ability to achieve. Once an objective has been achieved, it ceases to hold interest and the search is on for a new challenge.

Such people seek to rise to positions of power and responsibility, and are frequently found in general management, or in positions where their ability to keep the big picture in focus is critical. Their route to these positions may often be through – but is not confined to – sales, since they are natural entrepreneurs and want to know: 'What's in it for me?'

Suggested way of communicating with dominant types

Keep conversation short and to the point and be well prepared; use positive, simple but assertive language. Do not be intimidated by their abrupt manner, but demonstrate that you are interested in achieving similar goals.

Influence

Someone whose primary drive is influencing, as the name implies, is outgoing and gregarious. They genuinely like people and consequently have a strong, innate need to be liked. They will work hard to maintain harmony and are able to integrate and lead others using persuasion and enthusiasm. Such people are empathetic and seem able to understand what others are feeling without effort. These people respond very positively to peer-group recognition and, though they consider themselves as team-oriented, they are only really interested in leading the team. However, they will also be concerned at the effect that decisions they make will have on their colleagues' view of them.

Influencers will often be found working in environments that require communication and persuasive ability, so they are often found in – but are not confined to – public relations, advertising and sales.

Suggested ways of communicating with influencers

Allow time for them to express their thoughts and be interested in the way they feel. Be enthusiastic and appreciative of their ideas and, where appropriate, let them lead the team.

Stability

Someone whose primary drive is to be stable and steady (often referred to as an 'amiable') is deliberate in thought and action. Such people want to know before acting and therefore ask many 'why' questions. Reserved but amiable, such people inspire trust but are unlikely to reciprocate that trust until the other person has proven themselves worthy of it. This is not likely to happen easily or quickly. They are long-term planners, who prefer to try to avoid problems rather than confront them and are intensely loyal to those considered friends. Such people are careful and need to know that they are an integral and valued part of the team. Amiables dislike sudden unannounced change and prefer a cyclical element in their work. Amiables will frequently be found working in logistical and administrative roles or environments that require long-term commitment and continuity.

Suggested way of communicating with stable amiables

Answer all of their questions, no matter how irrelevant they may seem to you. Give time for thought and be absolutely sincere in your dealings with them.

Compliance

People whose primary drive is compliance are accurate, precise, detail-oriented and concerned for criteria or rules and fear chaos. Such people will often be highly qualified in more than one discipline. Analytical, sceptical and objective, they can be demanding and are often uncompromising about standards. Such people frequently have an odd sense of humour that is quite happy to let the 'know it all' talk about subjects that they really know little about and gently prick the 'know it all's' balloon.

Compliant types will often be found in work that requires knowledge and expertise, and a rigorous, analytical ability to assess facts and data. They are unlikely to make statements that cannot be backed up by facts and often take the stance 'prove it to me'.

Suggested ways of communicating with compliant types

Be prepared, know your facts and expect to answer many penetrating questions. Also, be prepared to prove your thoughts and ideas with data that can be checked.

Have you identified your own dominant way of communicating?

_____

_____

_____

Do you communicate differently in different situations?

_____

_____

_____

Can you use the suggested communication modes with anyone you know?

_____

_____

_____

Record any comments below.

_____

_____

_____

_____

_____

_____

HERRMANN BRAIN DOMINANCE INSTRUMENT

In the United States, Ned Herrmann, a senior manager at General Electric in the 1970s, also became interested in teams and groups and in why it was that certain teams were more creative than others. He observed that some teams would get on well but might not be as innovative as those who approached a problem with a diverse mixture of approaches.

He researched extensively into the recent discoveries of the workings of the human brain and developed a profile that indicates that there are four distinct thinking preferences, related to specific areas of the brain. He discovered this through the use of EEG measurements of brain waves, attached to the brain, which demonstrated which area of the brain was activated in different tasks.

He applied research already carried out by Paul MacLean (Chief of Brain Evolution and Behaviour at the National Institute of Mental Health in the

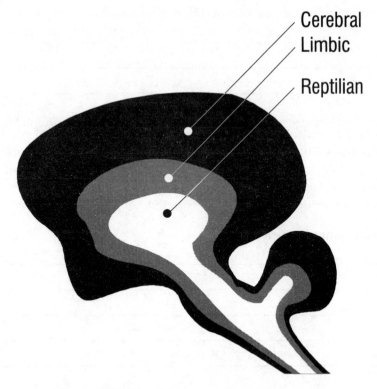

Cerebral
Limbic
Reptilian

Figure 11.1 *The triune brain*

United States) who developed the concept of the 'triune brain'. His research indicated that the human brain consisted of three layers, each layer physiologically and chemically different and corresponding to a stage in human evolution. Each layer is responsible for different kinds of mental processing.

As you can see from Figure 11.1, the reptilian brain was the earliest to develop and drives our instincts and survival mechanisms. The middle, limbic, layer deals with emotion and sequence, playing a key role in memory transformation and retrieval. The neocortex, or cerebral system, as we have mentioned before, is the most recent to develop and enables humans to think, perceive and speak.

Coupled with Roger Sperry's research at the California Institute of Technology into the left and right hemisphere activities of the cortical system, Ned Herrmann has developed a profile of questions that obviates the need to attach people to machines and can identify thinking preferences through a series of questions. This is referred to as the Herrmann Brain Dominance Instrument (HBDI).

The cortical area of the human brain has two somewhat separate functions. As you can see from Figure 11.2, the left area of the brain predominantly operates the logical, numerical, linguistic and orderly functions. The right area of the brain operates the global, rhythmic, imaginative functions.

The four thinking preferences are depicted in Figure 11.3. As you can see, the upper (cerebral) left A mode of thinking can be described as analytical, mathematical, technical and problem-solving. The lower (limbic) left B can be described as controlled, conservative, planned, organized and administrative in nature. The lower (limbic) right C is the interpersonal, emotional, musical, spiritual and the 'talker' modes, and the upper (cerebral) right D is the imaginative, synthesizing, artistic, holistic and conceptual modes.

The Herrmann research complements the DiSC profile but measures different aspects of a person. DiSC measures personality whereas Herrmann measures thinking preference. Each profile therefore enables you to get insights into who you are, how you think and how that affects your behaviour. You will naturally have some capability within each

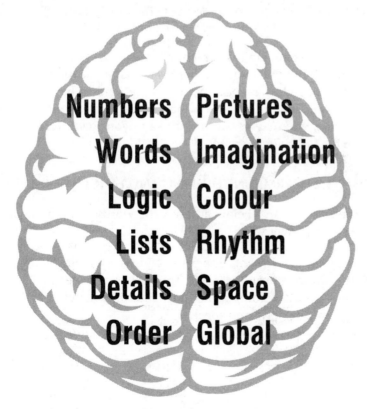

Figure 11.2   *The brain's hemispheres and their functions*

ANALYSE   **SYNERGIZE**

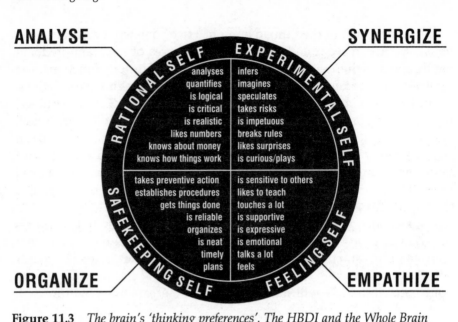

ORGANIZE   **EMPATHIZE**

Figure 11.3 *The brain's 'thinking preferences'. The HBDI and the Whole Brain Model are trademarks of the Ned Herrmann Group 1999*

quadrant of the Herrmann Instrument but you may find that there is one area of thinking in which you are happiest. Just as people have a dominance in left- or right-handedness, so people tend to have a dominant mode of thinking. It is not possible to include the whole of the HBDI in this book. However, you may get an insight as to your own thinking preferences from the following exercise.

EXERCISE 11.2 HERRMANN THINKING AND LANGUAGE INDICATOR

Look at the lists of words below and tick the words you most commonly use in your own conversation.

A	B	C	D
Accountable	Activist	Belong	Adaptable
Accurate	Applied	Care	Anticipate
Analytical	Assignment	Celebrate	Big Picture
Capitalization	Boundary	Coaching	Breaking rules
Competition	Bureaucracy	Communicate	Change
Focused	Caution	Cooperate	Conceptual
Invest	Controlled	Courage	Creative
Leverage	Credit	Employees	Design
Numbers	Dominant	Encourage	Different
Perform	Evaluate	Grass roots	Diverse

A	B	C	D
Power	Examine	Harmonious	Dynamic
Pricing	Forge	Interactive	Enhance
Rational	Framework	Mentoring	Enterprise
Reality	Insurance	Partnering	Explore
Research	Integrity	Relationships	Holistic
Revenue	Meticulous	Satisfaction	Long-term
Reward	Operations	Self-esteem	Sales
Standard	Proactive	Teamwork	Synthesizer
Technical	Prudent	Understand	Vision
Validation	Tenacious		

Total the number of ticks in each column and see whether you have a dominance in one particular area of thinking.

Study the example of an individual profile carried out recently, in Figure 11.4.

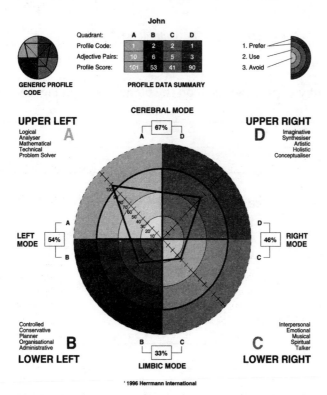

Figure 11.4 *Sample Herrmann Brain Dominance Profile for an individual*

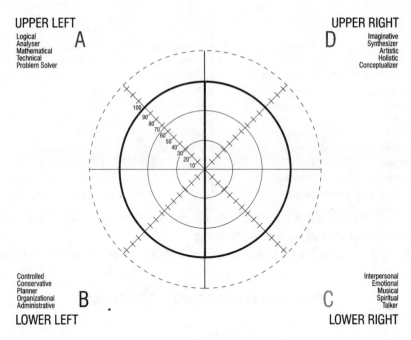

Figure 11.5   *Sample Herrmann Brain Dominance Profile*

Where might you place yourself on the blank profile in Figure 11.5?

_____

_____

_____

Where might you place your immediate colleagues?

_____

_____

_____

Where might you place your closest clients?

_____

_____

_____

PREFERENCE VERSUS CAPABILITY

As the Herrmann measures thinking preferences, it does not mean that you do not have excellent capabilities in all four quadrants. For example, you may have a preference to think creatively but have been trained to think analytically. You may have chosen a career path that did not reflect your preference but seemed to be an attractive route earlier in your life. As we mentioned earlier, people can go into careers as a result of parental pressure or economic need.

It is likely, however, that you will perform more effectively in activities linked to your preferred quadrant. You will have to take a more conscious and systematic decision to address other areas of thinking activity.

Inevitably this has an impact on teamwork and it is advisable to profile your whole team, or indeed your whole organization, to assess overall strengths and weaknesses of thinking. It sharpens up the general approach to work when people know which areas they need to address. Also, understanding and accepting why another person thinks differently to oneself can dramatically improve relationships.

We were working with a small team in an account management department where there had been misunderstanding and unexpressed frustration. When we profiled the individuals within the team it became clear that they came from very different viewpoints. Placing the team on a quadrant profile, we could demonstrate that one individual preferred analytical thinking, another organizational thinking and the third creativity. This had created problems of misunderstanding, as the language each of them used, and the perspectives and priorities they had, were very different. It had been difficult for them to find a common ground on which to work.

When they saw their profiles and understood one another better, it became easier for them to value the different ideas and contributions of other team members. They realized that it stimulated more creativity to come at a problem from several different angles rather than for them all to be looking at their work situations from the same angle. After this experience, they reported that this information had enhanced their team and that they were now 'working from a completely different playing field'.

Thinking preference also affects performance. If you do not enjoy doing something, you tend to procrastinate and put it off, or delegate it. Alternatively, you do the task but do not enjoy it, and so become bad tempered. For example, you may have noticed people who do not enjoy doing their expenses at the end of each month. They put it off until the very last moment when it is due and then carry out the activity as fast as they can to get it over with. Others hate filing, and papers pile up in filing trays in their office until they are eventually forced to take action. You may be able to think of work activities you do not enjoy and how this affects your ability to complete those tasks.

The Herrmann profile can be extremely insightful when working to develop teams. Not only does it help people to understand themselves and communicate better, it can also shed light on performance indicators. For example, we were working with a project management team recently who were having difficulty sustaining the momentum of their projects. The initial introduction of projects was no problem and the projects themselves were formulated through excellent analytical thinking processes. However, when handed over to other departments for implementation, the process would slow down and sometimes grind to a halt.

We were called in to help develop the team and, in passing, the senior manager mentioned the problem they were experiencing with integrating projects into other departments of the organization. When we did the group profile (see Figure 11.6), it became apparent that there was no one in the existing team who really enjoyed sequential thinking and organization.

The dominant preference of the team was in quadrant A (analytical), with the secondary preference in quadrant D (creative). The predominant mode of thinking was therefore cerebral (eg, they were more interested in

Example of group in A-D Cerebral Quadrants

10 Individuals

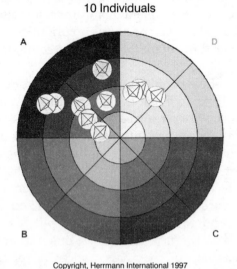

Figure 11.6 *Sample Herrmann Brain Dominance Profile for a group*

ideas and concepts than in people issues). Without a strong preference for quadrant B (organizational and procedural thinking) there was no one who got excited about finishing the job. Nor was there anyone who understood how to motivate people in order to get their clients in other departments to enthusiastically adopt and sustain the projects they initiated. The team were therefore excellent at analytical thinking and problem-solving. They were also good at thinking creatively around a problem. They were less good at step-by-step implementation.

When this team had been through the Herrmann process, they began to understand themselves better. They came to realize why some people found it difficult to understand and communicate with other people. They also came to realize why they were having this problem integrating their projects. When they looked at their recruitment policy, they also understood that they were hiring people who were excellent at quadrant A (thinking) but were not attracting people with quadrant B (organizational) or quadrant C (interpersonal) preferences.

Fortunately, you can develop other quadrants of thinking. As you understand how the brain connections are created, you can take practical

A Facts	**Future D**
Efficiency, financials, technology, past trends, performance, measurements, goals-objectives	Competition, environment, future trends, new concepts, national-world, vision-purpose, long-term strategy
Methods-regulations, quality and perfection risk reduction, resources, control, timing, policy	Training-development, teams-relationships, community relations, customer relations, communications, culture-values, recognition
B Form	**Feeling C**

Figure 11.7 *Herrmann Brain Dominance Instrument 'walkabout'*

measures to develop new ways of thinking. Once a team or an individual has become aware of their least preferred thinking activities, they can introduce systems to ensure that they do not neglect more lateral perspectives. For decision-making or problem-solving, it is possible to use a model to focus attention on the priorities and issues of each quadrant one by one. See Figure 11.7.

This is particularly useful for making presentations, as any presentation will need to incorporate the language and priorities of each quadrant. You can sometimes assess your audience and shape the presentation in their language. At other times you may not know the thinking preferences of your audience and will need to include each quadrant in your presentation. For example, a presentation should include the global overview and creative vision (D), facts, figures and graphs (A), step-by-step information where details are chunked down into manageable groups (B), and input about the implications of the information on the people involved (C).

The Herrmann profile can be regarded as a reference point to branch out from rather than as a box in which to sit. Developing different areas of your brain's thinking capacity can give you new perspectives and enable you to see situations in a new light. This broadening of outlook can influence your strategy, recruitment and teamwork, as well as your personal ability to perform and communicate.

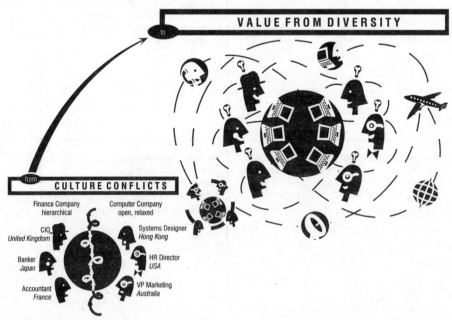

Figure 11.8 *Cultural Diversity Map*

THE DIFFERENCE BETWEEN MEN AND WOMEN

The entrance of women into the workplace in the last half of the twentieth century has influenced working practices and has resulted in radical changes to society as a whole. Prior to the 1950s, organizations were almost entirely male preserves. Organizational culture and routines assumed the member of staff would have someone at home to cater and care for the family. Nowadays men and women are having to learn to share responsibilities. Organizations have begun to offer flexible hours, crèches and paid maternity and paternity leave.

These changes demand that both men and women adopt new modes of behaviour. With communication being the key to the successful performance of an organization today, the way men and women communicate with each other in business has thus become a critical skill.

What has recently come to light to help us bridge the gender gap of communication is research showing that the male and female brains are physiologically different. This difference leads to thinking and behavioural preferences in much the same way as the Herrmann profiles we discussed above. In fact, the Herrmann group profiles also demonstrate this difference, as you will see from the male group and female group profiles shown in Figure 11.9.

Research has shown that the right and left cortical areas of the brain are interconnected by a network of nerves known as the *corpus callosum*. The *corpus callosum* appears to be more dense in women than in men, demonstrating a closer interconnection between the two sides of the brain. These differences are generated in the womb as the brain of the foetus develops and male and female brains are flooded with different hormones. Inevitably, there are variations in this development and not all women are typically 'female', nor all men typically 'male'. Nonetheless, research is showing that there are some fundamental differences in the majority of male and female brains. These physical differences result in different sets of behaviours and drives.

Ann and Bill Moir, in their book, *Why Men Don't Iron*, have recently highlighted the research that has been done in this area. This suggests that the closer interconnection between both sides of the brain results in women, when they are discussing an issue, seeing many different aspects to it, where a man is inclined to focus on what he believes to be the key points. Men tend to focus single-mindedly on a problem and be good at problem analysis; women tend to be good at problem understanding. Putting the two perspectives together can lead to a more holistic way of reaching solutions – or to misunderstanding! (see Figure 11.10)

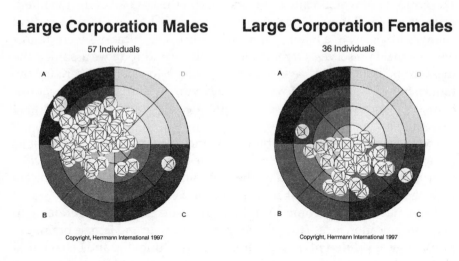

Figure 11.9   *Sample Herrmann Brain Dominance Profiles for men and women*

Figure 11.10   *An unfortunate result of male and female brain physiology*

A woman's neural connections appear to give her an advantage in linguistic skills. Under stress, a man appears to get a stronger 'fight or flight' response. Therefore, at moments of conflict a woman is more likely to attempt to talk her way out of it; a man is more likely to become aggressive or to walk out.

Hormones play a part in these responses. The female brain has more serotonin, which acts as a brake and moderator on behaviour; the male brain has more testosterone and androgens, which act as an accelerator. While the influences of society cannot be removed from the picture, these physical differences can explain many of the misunderstandings at work. We are talking here in generalities, but suspect that many readers will be able to think of instances where the different responses of men and women have been apparent in varying approaches and priorities. To value this diversity can lead to enhanced understanding and improved relationships at work. Many of the men and women with whom we work express confusion and frustration at the difficulties they experience in communicating with groups of the opposite sex.

The trend is set for more women to enter the workplace. It is estimated that in the next ten years the workforce in the UK will increase by 1.5 million, of which 85 per cent will be women. This is having an influence on the communication culture of businesses, and some men are feeling threatened by these changes. British Petroleum and the NatWest Bank are introducing training courses for men, helping them to develop their communication and teamworking abilities.

Women, on the other hand, have other difficulties. Many report that they find it difficult to be 'heard' in meetings. They express an idea and the male group with whom they work either do not notice it or reject it. Some weeks later, one of the males present introduces that same idea as if it were his own.

In the organization of the future, men and women need to find a 'third way' of communicating which allows them to see one another 'anew'. Past modes of communicating are no longer appropriate. Women need to learn to express themselves honestly and assertively at work. They also need support with the different pressures of home and work and the changes these are introducing into previously male work cultures. At the moment many women are frightened to admit that they need to leave work for childcare reasons. Companies with a 'family-friendly' approach are introducing crèches, flexi-hours and policies to manage time taken to care for sick children. This eases the burden for both men and women in the support of family needs.

Men need to be able to value the insights and different perspectives that the female brings to work. An all-male or all-female board of directors will not have the diversity of thought necessary to take that organization forward. Wherever possible, board rooms and teams should be populated by members of both sexes. Without this mixture of thought and experience a company is only getting a limited and one-sided view of any situation.

Both men and women experience challenges in plotting their career path. In the past a man often thought of a straight career path through one profession and even within one organization. This is unlikely to be his experience today. A woman was often brought up to think she would 'work until' she had children and did not necessarily have a long-term view of her career. Women are now returning to work a few weeks after childbirth and others are opting not to have children in favour of working. Women are breaking through the glass ceiling, albeit slowly, to senior positions.

Things are certainly not what they were. It is likely that whether you are a man or a woman you may choose to change career several times during your lifetime. The ability to understand yourself, your personality and your thinking preferences will help you in making these decisions. It will help you to identify areas of activity you enjoy and excel at.

This helps you to define your own 'brand' of excellence. It will also help you to develop good working relationships with the people with whom you come into contact. All of this gives you choice and a feeling of personal power. It is easier to feel in control of your destiny when you are aware of your own strengths and the choices available to you.

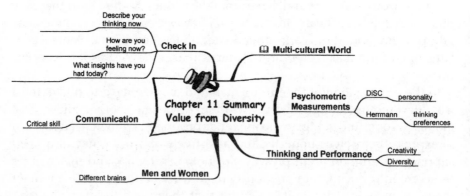

Figure 11.11 *Summary: value from diversity*

12

Brain-to-Brain Communication

All human brains have the same design. When you understand how thought patterns and connections are produced and how and why everyone is different in their approach to work, it is easier to have human-to-human, brain-to-brain and, indeed, heart-to-heart contact. This is to gain true value from diversity.

Most communication problems occur through your expectations of how you want the other person to respond. If you can enjoy and work with the differences, communication is transformed into a continuous learning experience and can take on a sense of adventure, in which all those involved can feel validated. As the human brain is still the most complex system known to mankind, it is hardly surprising that the workings of someone else's brain should remain something of a mystery.

LANGUAGE

Language is, of course, an important indicator of how someone is feeling about themselves or about a situation. Sharpen your ear to notice the kind of words you are using both internally in your thoughts and externally when you speak to other people. There are many direct and indirect clues that help you to interpret the emotion or hidden goals behind the main message. What are sometimes called 'Freudian slips' can speak volumes.

You can shape your language to make another person feel comfortable. Many people find it difficult to accept praise or success and shrug it off with a derogatory remark about themselves, or say 'it was just luck'. This could well be a sign that the person has low self-esteem. You often notice people saying 'I'm no good at French/singing/drawing'. This could either be because they do not feel confident at a skill or be because they feel very confident but do not want to be accused of 'showing off'. As we have said before, cultural norms vary regarding expressions of personal success or achievement. If people are competing in a global environment, they need to become aware of these differences. If Americans, for example, are happy to share their achievements without embarrassment, then it is probably advisable for other nationalities such as the British to learn to do so too. Alternatively, people may assume that they are not as competent as their US colleagues. To continue to promote your personal 'brand', become more aware of how you are expressing yourself.

Speaking negatively about something one is trying to achieve sabotages efforts to reach goals. It is noticeable how many people say 'I am hopeless at remembering names and faces' even though this language statement directly contradicts their goal, which is to remember people's names.

The ability to accept praise or critical feedback is an integral part of becoming confident, mature and assertive. It demonstrates an ability to accept that there is always scope to learn from others and to value their input even if, as in the case of criticism, it can sometimes appear to be hurtful. When giving or receiving criticism at work, it is helpful to remember that it is behaviour that is under question, not the person themselves. Telling someone they are 'stupid' or have 'failed' is very different from telling them that you would have preferred them to act or do something differently.

LISTENING

Listening can be difficult and we are seldom taught how to do it effectively. Your brain has a relatively short attention span unless you are interactively involved. Most meetings that are set up fail to interest the majority of people attending them, as it is frequently the case that one person does most of the talking and others sit around listening. Whilst they listen, they may well be thinking about something else altogether – their next meeting, the piles of work on their desk, what they need to buy at the supermarket, etc.

Learning to listen carefully to another person is an art. It also has a bottom-line effect: resources of both time and money are often wasted when a message is miscommunicated. It is therefore dangerous to assume that a person means the same as you think they do – their understanding of a word or an issue might be completely different to your own. Each one of us has a unique understanding and experience of life and language.

One way to immediately enhance your ability to listen is to build mind pictures of the information to which you are listening. The brain builds mind pictures of information and experience and stores them in your long-term memory. Your memory works through your five senses, taking in information through sight, sound, touch, taste and smell. When you think back to school days, or your first job, you may recall a series of pictures relating to places and people; you may also remember what it felt like to be there, and the voices, sounds, smells and tastes that accompanied the experience. The more you can involve your senses, through memory and imagination, when you listen, the better you are able to involve yourself with the information.

Creating the mental pictures of the information helps you to listen. For example, if a lawyer is talking about a case, you can imagine what the people and events they are describing might look like. If you work in a highway planning department, you might imagine the roads and the builders who are building them; if you are working in a financial department, you might imagine currency being handed from one person to another. If there are gaps in your picture, ie missing pieces, ask questions until you have a complete picture. We term this the 'complete picture method'.

Clarifying questions, such as 'is this what I heard you say?', help you to be involved. Paraphrasing what you heard in your own language helps you to drive the message home in your own mind and also ascertains that you have listened accurately. The more specific you can be, the better.

When you communicate at work, do you give the other person time to finish what they are trying to say? Or do you get impatient to try to put your own point of view? Do you give them time to express what they want or need? Introverted people, for example, take longer to process information, as they need to reflect carefully upon what they have heard and what they want to say. Extroverted people will work out their thoughts through language, rather than internally. If you are an extrovert, you may not be giving introverts enough time to frame what they want to say. If you are an introvert, you may find yourself threatened by the faster pace of an extrovert.

The human brain has a habit of completing gaps of information. This is why messages often become garbled, as each person listening to the same speaker will be filling the gaps and interpreting them in their own way, through their own priorities and experience. If you hear the phrase 'Mary had a little. . .' you may automatically think of a word to complete the gap. Consider how often people make assumptions as to what is being said, without clarifying the true meaning that was intended. There are, after all, several versions of the 'Mary had a little lamb' rhyme.

If you have a soft voice it can be difficult for people to pick up what you are saying. Whilst they can ask you to repeat yourself once or twice, they will eventually get too bored or embarrassed to continue to do so. They may switch off their minds and think of something different. At this point their brains will be filling in the gaps. If you are aware that your voice is soft, learn to project it by throwing it to the furthest point and the furthest person in the room. Surprisingly enough, you can change the tone and strength of your voice just through thinking differently and focusing on the place you would like it to reach. Try it at your next meeting.

Many people complain that they lack the ability to concentrate. There is some evidence that men find it harder to listen than women. You can enhance your listening skills through focus exercises. For example, as you read this book, allow your ears to tune in to any sounds there are around you. There may be people talking, you may hear the sound of the page turning, cars outside, birds, wind, etc. Every so often during a day, when you are in your office or walking along the street, consider how many different sounds you can register. These exercises will help you to remain focused when listening to someone talking to you at a meeting or presentation.

BUILDING RELATIONSHIPS

The trend at work has moved towards the development of small teams who come together for a short period of time in order to implement a specific project. In such cases it is important to be able to build relationships as fast as possible with team members in order to be able to work effectively together to get the job done.

Building rapport starts through attention to the other person. One school of thought claims you can build instant rapport by noticing how people stand or sit and, as far as possible, mirroring their positions, body language and pace of speech. Do not mimic precisely and avoid any individual traits such as stuttering. Use your sensitivity to make them feel comfortable. Notice also how the person processes information by becoming aware of the language they use to represent their experiences and then, as far as is possible, match your language to theirs. This will enable the other person to feel more comfortable, relaxed and open in your company. For example:

1. *Visual*: a person who processes experiences visually may use such words as 'the outlook is bright', 'do you see what I mean?' or 'do you get the picture?' You may also notice that their eyes move upwards as they remember and construct images in their head.
2. *Auditory*: a person who processes experiences auditorally may use such words as 'they're not on my wavelength', 'she's chirpy this morning' or 'I'd say we are in tune on that'. You may also notice that their eyes move sideways as they remember and construct sounds and voices in their head.
3. *Kinaesthetic*: a person who processes experiences kinaesthetically may use such words as 'I feel moved by the weight of all this pressure', 'he's a pushy so-and-so' or 'I stand firm on that statement'. You may also notice that their eyes move downwards as they feel experiences they are remembering or imagining.

Can you think how you process information? Next time you are at a meeting, tune in to the language of your colleagues and see if you can hear any words that identify how people are interpreting their world.

With this information and with the communication and thinking styles profiling mentioned in the previous chapter, your ability to understand and relate to other people can be dramatically enhanced. Practise with it on a daily basis and become aware of what is working and what is not working. Try to understand the other person's point of view and accept that they have a right to that viewpoint even if it is contrary to your own.

Many projects fail as a result of the people-conflicts within a team, where egos clash and others in the team may be afraid to express themselves. In a recent business school survey it was estimated that a large company they were working with was losing as much as US $4 million a year through projects that were not implemented. They identified performance indicators for successful projects and were able to put much of this success down to the project manager's behaviour. Personal responsibility, integrity and communication skills were the key to success. The ability to be truthful and realistic about targets and progress developed trust within the team and also with clients. Creativity was another key success factor as it was proved to be important to find other ways of approaching tasks by thinking 'out of the box'.

Effective communication is therefore a critical part of good business practice and has bottom-line results. It can help you in many other areas of your life too. People we have worked with have frequently reported that their private lives have been enhanced by sharing the information they have gained at work with partners and children.

COMMUNICATING CONFIDENTLY

Much has been written about assertiveness. People often confuse it with aggressiveness. In the examples below, you will find descriptions of four categories of behaviour that you may have encountered at work. Notice where you fit in and where some of your colleagues, clients and team members might fit in. You need to be careful not to put people into boxes – each one of us is unique – but understanding the fears and drives behind the behaviour can often help you to work with the person rather than to allow the differences to cause misunderstandings.

COMMON BEHAVIOURAL TYPES

Passive or non-assertive ('You're OK, I'm not OK')

- A person who is timid, unselfconfident and finds it hard to stand up for themselves. These people can get what they want indirectly by making others feel sorry for them or protective. They tend to become victims or martyrs. They do not know when to say 'no' and are malleable to other people's whims and demands.
- Body language: hunched shoulders, downcast eyes, quiet voice, crossed legs when standing.
- Words/phrases: perhaps; maybe; I wonder if you could; I'm hopeless; it's not important; never mind.

Passive aggressive or indirectly aggressive ('You're not OK, I'm not OK')

- A person who is passive aggressive acts in what appears to be a passive manner whilst feeling aggressive and often thinking 'I'll get my revenge later'. Their inability to express their anger or resentment directly can result in their being able to manipulate other people to do what they want through emotional blackmail.

- Body language: this is a very good example of how body language often speaks louder than words. They may agree verbally that they are happy to do a job but their emotional body language will demonstrate clearly that they are not happy to do it. Emotions are infectious.
- Words/phrases: perhaps; maybe; I wonder if you could; I'm hopeless; it's not important; never mind.

Aggressive ('I'm OK, you're not OK')

- A person who is aggressive gets what they want through verbal or physical threat or force. They do not care about the rights of others and consider that they are right, not caring what other people think or want and tending to blame them. Their aggressive and bullying manner can often result in other people feeling humiliated and resentful towards them and attacking back in some more indirect way later.
- Body language: pointing finger, sharp, firm sarcastic voice; leans forward.
- Words/phrases: you'd better; don't be stupid; your fault; you should/ought/must.

Assertive ('I'm OK, you're OK')

- A person who is assertive respects their own rights and the rights of others. They seek a working compromise rather than a win. They express themselves directly without being aggressive. Such people have a sense of self-worth and allow other people to have different opinions but can put their own opinion calmly and openly.
- Body language: relaxed; good eye contact; not hostile; collaborative.
- Words/phrases: 'I' statements; we could; let's; what do you think?; how do you feel about this?

Can you think of people you work with who fall into these categories? Have you found some of their behaviours difficult to manage? Do you find yourself behaving differently when you are with them?

EXERCISE 12.1 MATCH AND MANAGE

1. Think of certain people you work with who fall into these categories and list them below, you might like to use a code name for security reasons!

Name	Behaviours difficult to manage

2. Against each of their names, list the behaviours you find difficult to manage.

3. Do you find yourself behaving differently when you are with them? If 'yes', state how below.

_____

_____

_____

_____

_____

_____

To develop better relationships with other people it can be helpful to examine your own behaviour and make any changes that you feel might be appropriate. You can seldom change other people, but by changing your own behaviour you will find that, like altering your steps in a dance, they will change their behaviour too. If you start to dance the waltz, it is difficult for them to continue to dance the tango!

EXERCISE 12.2 UPDATE

It is important not to judge the person by their behaviours. You develop behavioural traits as a way of protecting yourself as you grow up and through life experiences.

1. Are your current behaviours still helpful and appropriate to the outcomes you want in your life? List below a few behaviours that you believe are not serving you well.

_____

_____

_____

_____

_____

_____

2. How might you want to change those behaviours?

_____

_____

_____

_____

_____

BEING ASSERTIVE

Assertiveness is one of the most empowering skills to acquire. It can transform your relationships within a very short time. Take an honest look at yourself as you answer Exercise 12.3.

EXERCISE 12.3 HOW ASSERTIVE ARE YOU?

Mark the following statements between 0–10 according to your own assessment of how you are behaving at the moment.
How effective are you at:

1. Both respecting yourself and giving respect to others?
2. Taking responsibility for yourself, including the recognition that you have a responsibility towards others?

3. Expressing needs, wants and feelings without punishing other people or violating their rights?
4. Being direct and honest in your communication with others?
5. Recognizing you have a number of rights which you can use and defend?
6. Getting a clearer picture of how you feel and seeing these feelings as important?
7. Expressing yourself clearly, simply and directly but still in your own way?
8. Not putting others down or being bossy?
9. Being able to say no, or that you don't understand?
10. Challenging situations which exclude you or others from taking part on an equal basis?
11. Being clear about what you want to accomplish, giving consideration to your feelings and then being prepared to negotiate in a responsible way?
12. Negotiating changes with others on an equal basis of power rather than trying to win?
13. Allowing yourself to make mistakes?
14. Allowing yourself to enjoy successes?
15. Allowing yourself to change your mind or take time over a decision?
16. Asking clearly for what you want?

Now add up the scores. These reflect your own assessment of your present assertiveness levels. If you scored less than 90 you may need to practise the assertiveness techniques that follow. These will help you to manage difficult situations in the future. If you scored more than 90 you are aware of the principles of assertiveness – are your practising them?

ASSERTIVENESS TECHNIQUES

Of all the methods developed to communicate assertively, the Three-Step Model is one of the simplest and most effective. Before attempting any new technique, it is essential you define a positive outcome that moves you away from a problem and towards a solution. Always define the positive outcome for each challenging situation that you face.

THE THREE-STEP MODEL

- Step One: Actively listen to what the other person is saying and demonstrate that you have heard and understood.
- Step Two: Say what you think rationally about the situation and what you are feeling.
- Step Three: Say what you want to happen.

Use link words such as 'however' or 'and' rather than 'but'. For example, in negotiating priorities:

- Step One: 'I understand that you need this report by tomorrow morning.'
- Step Two: 'However, I have another important project I have to complete.'
- Step Three: 'And I suggest I try to get the report to you by early afternoon.'

In handling customer complaints:

- Step One: 'I understand that you are concerned about this.'
- Step Two: 'I would be upset too if this happened to me.'
- Step Three: 'Let me call my factory and get back to you by 4 pm with an answer.'

The essential part of assertive behaviour is taking responsibility for your own response to a situation. For example: 'When you ask me to take work home I feel angry, so could we please talk about it?' Another person may not feel angry about taking work home and therefore the anger is your own personal response.

The key is always to focus on behaviour and not personality. For example, not saying 'You are inconsiderate' but 'When you constantly interrupt, I feel that you are not taking me into consideration. Could we look at making some changes?'

Whenever the situation requires that you act assertively, ensure that your thinking is positive, rational and constructive. Take whatever time you need before you respond: do not allow yourself to feel rushed. Clarify the situation and consider what it is you really want and how you can work together with the other person.

Notice your own language and change it to support your goals and your own sense of control over events. Use 'I' statements whenever possible;

change 'can't' to 'choose not to' where applicable; change 'need' to 'want'; change 'have to' to 'choose to'; change 'should' to 'could'.

Avoid blame by changing sentences from passive into active: for example, from 'you are making me angry' to 'when you interrupt me I feel angry', taking responsibility for your own reaction.

Begin to adopt the physiology and language of an assertive person and integrate it into your life every day. You may need to remind yourself to do this by wearing your watch on the opposite wrist for a period of time. Each time you look at your watch, remind yourself to stand taller, more open and relaxed and develop positive and confident thoughts and behaviour.

If you have had a tendency to aggression, take a deep breath before speaking and relax your shoulders; if you have had a tendency to be passive, pull yourself up straighter and feel the strength and firmness of your spine. When you combine physiology with supportive thoughts you will find that your emotional state becomes easier to manage and that your behaviour will naturally become more assertive.

PROBLEM RELATIONSHIP PATTERNS AT WORK

In assertive communication you are treating other people as equals. Everyone at work is an adult. Consider whether you are communicating on an adult-to-adult basis at work. You are treating other people as children if you either shield them from difficult facts or feelings or tell them what to do in the manner of an authority figure to a child. Whilst there may be differences of status and hierarchy existing within your organization, the more you can behave to others on an adult-to-adult basis, the more you help yourself and others to accept responsibility for the situations that occur.

A common imbalance occurs when one person – usually but not always a superior figure – adopts a critical or authoritarian-style role of 'I know best' and the other person adapts their behaviour to avoid the criticism and gain the approval of the critic. This adapted behaviour tends to be more child-like, blaming the other person and not taking responsibility in an adult way for the communication process. This situation can equally happen if the person who thinks he or she 'knows best' is over-protective or over-nurturing.

When these situations arise, it can set up a triangle whereby the critical figure becomes perceived, rightly or wrongly, as a *persecutor* and the adapted figure becomes a *victim* and can blame the other person for their problems. The victim is often too intimidated to discuss their feelings and needs with the persecutor and so turns to a *rescuer*, generally a peer, to share their frustrations and pain. In this way the true nature of the problem is disguised and issues are not discussed in an open or honest manner. This simply perpetuates the problem; emotions build up and one of the parties can sometimes explode.

EXERCISE 12.4 THE PERPETUAL TRIANGLE

Consider the persecutor–victim–rescuer model, and write down any thoughts you have about work situations where this happens:

_____

_____

_____

_____

_____

_____

Once again, the way out of the triangle is to identify a positive solution and devise a strategy to reach it. The key is for the victim and the persecutor to discuss their feelings and to agree a way forward that acknowledges both their points of view and benefits them. This means that all three people within the triangle need to adopt win–win assertive and adult behaviour. The 'persecutor' has to accept that the 'victim' is adult. The victim needs to accept that they are themself adult and feel free to express their needs and take responsibility for their own behaviour. The best option for the rescuer is to disentangle themself and leave the other two to work out a solution together.

You may have noticed this behaviour – corners of an office where people are gathering to moan about someone or some situation. The people involved are often getting energy from the negativity that is being shared.

Whether you are involved in this triangle yourself, or observe it in members of your team, it can be positively managed by helping each individual to feel supported in working towards a mutually agreed target.

(Derived from 'The Drama Triangle', developed by SB Karpman, copyright 1968 *Transactional Analysis Bulletin*, reproduced in Berne, Eric, *What Do You Say After You Say Hello?*, Corgi, 1990.)

INTERNATIONAL COMMUNICATION

A vast amount of communication is now conducted on a global scale. On these occasions creating value out of diversity is all the more important. Respecting and adapting to different cultures and practices becomes essential learning. Clarifying the understanding of language is vital. Be friendly on the telephone: you can hear when a person is smiling and well intentioned. Make sure any voicemail greeting is clear and welcoming. Practise improving the tone and quality of your voice if necessary.

One of the main channels of communication currently and for the future is via e-mail and the Internet. Even though it may appear to be a cold and technical method, it is perfectly feasible to build excellent teamworking and client relationships on-screen. Here are some suggestions:

- New software packages allow you to use colour, symbols and pictures in your e-mails.
- Be creative!
- Be conversational but clear and to the point.
- Beware of using capital letters as it is an over-forceful way of making a point.
- Read your message back and imagine how the person will receive it.
- Consider the time pressures, cultural festivals and other stresses that the reader is facing.

If you are working in a virtual team, include something personal at least once a week. Ask them how they are, what they have been doing socially that week, how their family is, etc. Build up mutual interest and consideration. Be aware who else might pick up your message: confidentiality is difficult on the web.

E-mail communication is fast and people expect speedy responses. Acknowledge mail and, if necessary, inform the person that you will get back to them with a reply later. Learning to touch-type can help you to speed up the process enormously. Computers are likely to be an increasingly frequent form of communication. The more you can adapt your own practices to meet this change, the more you will come to enjoy it.

THE POWER OF INTENTION

This chapter has posed a series of questions and theories about how people relate together. Assertiveness emphasizes the intrinsic and equal value of any two human beings, whatever their work status. It also reinforces the importance of each party having the intention to seek a win–win solution whenever possible.

Whatever part of the world we come from, we all have the same model of brain. It is easy to see, therefore, that the more you understand your own thoughts, intentions, fears, hopes and expectations, the more you will be able to understand those of other people. This is what we term brain-to-brain communication.

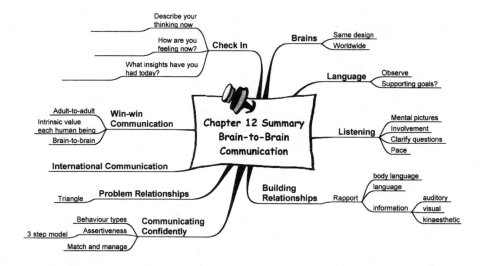

Figure 12.1 *Summary: brain-to-brain communication*

13

Meetings: The Engine of Your Business

Surveys demonstrate that less than 25 per cent of meetings result in effective actions being taken. With time at such a premium today, it is worth questioning the purpose and necessity of any meeting in which you are involved. Meetings can take up vital time. They are the engine of your business. Once you have the right techniques, culture and thinking systems in place, you have the potential to cut your meeting times by half. Consider now the part you are playing in the success of the meetings you attend.

The environment and layout of the room create an atmosphere for the style of meeting. People are affected by the place in which they work and will think and respond differently in one place or another. Consider the type of energy you want to create: for example, you may be looking for a different environment for a creative session compared to a budget meeting. What techniques and methodologies might support the work you are doing?

How do you invite people to a meeting? Who is critical to its success? Who might just come for a short time? Often people stay for the whole duration of a meeting when in fact they are only required to be there for certain agenda items.

Gain clarity, and focus the group on tangible and positive outcomes. Ensure that the meeting is framed with a positive title – people will arrive in a very different mood at a meeting entitled 'Building Team Spirit' to one entitled 'Rectifying Team Conflict'. Whatever the subject, having an agenda circulated beforehand helps people to consider their own feelings and input before the meeting.

Meetings can be emotional occasions – excitement, frustration, resentment, anger, boredom, fear, etc. Allow the expression of feelings. They will be part of the energy that is created between the people present and it is usually better to allow time for them to be discussed. Otherwise people continue to harbour their emotions without a safe outlet. As we discussed in Chapter 4, 'Emotional Intelligence', emotions need to be accepted and respected. Should you try to deny or rationalize someone out of a feeling, you may find that person sabotaging your efforts in other ways.

Be aware of this for yourself too. Meetings are an opportunity for you to shine. The energy you bring to a room as you walk in is tangible to those present. Emotions are infectious, so a positive attitude on the part of one person can soon generate a positive atmosphere throughout a meeting. Your successful future lies in the way people perceive you. Show people that you can manage yourself effectively in meetings and this will enhance your reputation through your organization and beyond.

A person talking at a meeting or presentation may be doing their best to make the information interesting. However, this does not mean to say that it will be interesting to those listening. It is therefore the responsibility of the listener, as much as the speaker, to shape the information in such a way as to keep their attention. Many people report 'this meeting is boring', without considering what they might personally do to make it more interesting and creative.

We have discussed some ways in which to make listening more memorable. This can be through maintaining eye contact with the person, or through taking notes or maps. It may be by suggesting more people become involved in the activities. Another technique, as we discussed in Chapter 12, is to allow your imagination to make interesting pictures or stories from the facts being given to you.

Take personal responsibility for keeping your own motivation and attention level high. Imagine your attention level on a gauge between 0 and 10, with 10 being highly attentive. Ensure that your energy towards the person speaking and the interaction between you and the group is above level 5. If you notice it slip below 5 do something to engage your mind with the information once more.

The next exercise gives you the opportunity to consider how your thinking affected your behaviour at a recent meeting.

EXERCISE 13.1 FOUR STEPS IN THINKING FOR MEETINGS

Behaviour influences bottom-line results. The close inter-relationship between thoughts, emotions and behaviour can be demonstrated through this model. Use this time to consider your response to a challenging situation that you have experienced in a meeting.

Note down:

1. A challenging situation you have faced in a meeting. Take a specific incident:

_____

_____

_____

2. The emotion you experienced when you faced this challenge:

_____

_____

_____

3. Expectations:

(a) What expectations did you have of yourself regarding the meeting (eg, 'I should/must get my point accepted'):

_____

_____

_____

(b) What expectations did you have regarding the other people involved in the meeting (eg, 'they should keep quiet' or 'they must agree to my point or I shall feel I have failed'):

_____

_____

_____

(c) What expectations do you have regarding meetings in general (eg, meetings should be focused):

_____

_____

_____

4. Feedback: When you look at the expectations you had of this situation, ask yourself whether they were rational and helpful to you. You can do this by questioning your thinking in the following way:

(a) Was your thinking rational? (Just because you would have preferred the meeting to be the way you wanted and expected, is it logical to believe that it must be that way?)

_____

_____

_____

(b) Would other people have had similar expectations of the meeting? (Would everyone respond to it in the same way as you?) If not, how else might you choose to respond in future when you think of how others respond?

_____

_____

_____

(c) Was your thinking helpful? (Was your thinking supporting you in the achievement of your desired goal?)

_____

_____

_____

(d) Note down what influence your thinking may have had on your own behaviour and the proceedings of the meeting in general:

_____

_____

_____

(e) What might be a more helpful way to think in future?

_____

_____

_____

How might your own behaviour be affecting other people? Remember that the brain likes to mimic other people and that you are a role model. As we spend a great deal of our time in meetings, it is important that you become aware of both how other people's behaviours and your own can affect the outcomes of that meeting.

How do you feel, for example, when it is your chance to speak and people start to fidget or whisper to each other? Do you find that people can be too nervous to tell you the truth and protect you with what they believe to be the answers you want to hear?

EXERCISE 13.2 BEHAVIOURAL ANALYSIS

At your next meeting, draw a diagram of the people sitting around the table, list their names and colour code each time they exhibit a behaviour, eg a red cross for negative comments, a blue tick for positive comments and a yellow circle for positive body language.

Each time a person speaks, draw an arrow to the person or persons addressed. If the person is speaking to everyone, draw the arrow to the centre of the table. If two people are exchanging quiet asides, put arrows between them.

These are just a few examples you can use. You will find this a fascinating study. You need only do it for a 10–20-minute period in order to gain insight into the group's behaviour dynamics.

THE ART OF FACILITATION

'The wise leader knows how to facilitate the unfolding group process, because the leader is also a process. The leader knows how to have a profound influence without making things happen. Facilitating what is happening is more potent than pushing for what you wish were happening.' (Lao Tzu, Chinese philosopher, 5th century BC)

Using facilitation skills transforms and speeds up meetings. Facilitation is about letting the group or team evolve a solution rather than telling them what you think the solution should be. Many managers walk into a meeting having already decided the outcome. They may give a pretence of listening to the comments of other people by saying at the beginning: 'I think we should do XYZ. What do you think?' People will nod and possibly agree, deferring to hierarchical status, but may well go away feeling resentful that they were not sufficiently involved. If you let a group evolve their own solution, you are more likely to get commitment that results in action.

You do this by:

- ensuring that everyone understands the goal you are seeking to achieve as a group;
- finding out what people are feeling about this goal;
- collecting people's views on business issues that influence this goal;
- getting individual and group creative suggestions regarding this goal;
- prioritizing issues and suggestions continually;
- allowing people to volunteer to commit to undertake these actions; and
- ensuring that there is a monitoring system to check when steps have been achieved.

The facilitator:

- asks questions;
- does not make statements;
- does not direct the group;
- encourages the group to contribute;
- encourages individuals to participate;
- ensures that no one is trampled on;
- keeps people focused; and
- leads the group towards a solution.

Rotating a facilitator or chairperson changes the dynamic of a meeting. Many routine meetings have the same person chairing them week after week. People sit in the same place around a table. Little cliques and factions develop within the main group. Be the instigator of change and inspire people to develop new ways of running meetings.

A common visual focus, such as a diagram, a whiteboard or a flipchart motivates people to work together and clarifies thinking and understanding as you progress. The mapping format used throughout this book works extremely well for recording information at meetings and allows people to see that their ideas have been noticed and recorded.

Working faster and more creatively prevents problems such as ego trips and ensures that ideas are developed without criticism. Finding ways of preventing the monopolization of input encourages quiet people to speak up. You may find that the person who has sat quietly in the corner for years has some nuggets for you.

If you reach an impasse, then suggest a break and reconvene. Much good work is done in the informal break periods between sessions. Many meetings go on far too long and after 60 minutes brains switch off. If you have a long agenda, make certain you build in five-minute breaks every 55 minutes. During these five-minute breaks you are allowing the attendees to consolidate what they have just heard. This is important if you want positive outcomes.

All the methods we have described enhance the effectiveness of meetings.

CASE STUDY 1

Carolyn Kilgariff, Compliance Manager of Barclays Bank Offshore Services, came on an Open Programme for her own personal development. Since that time she has used mapping and the concepts of whole-brain thinking for herself and for her team. She has found it helpful for planning, note-taking, brainstorming and structuring projects. In long conferences she found the thinking methods helped her to keep awake and pay attention as well as enabling her to store the information from one long day on one piece of paper. The information and skills have helped her to focus her mind. She is a working mother and therefore has to organize many different tasks.

The techniques have helped her communicate with her team and with other people around her. She finds that they now communicate more broadly and laterally and yet keep a focus on the task in hand. She says people make an effort to sit next to her in order to watch what she does – and steal her coloured pens. People cross the room at conferences to talk to her. She has therefore extended her network.

CASE STUDY 2

In 1994, we ran a three-day programme for Brian Fries, Vice-President of Project and Quality Management at the Chase Manhattan Bank, when he was setting up his Project and Quality Management team to integrate quality systems throughout Chemical Bank (as they were then). The workshop included Mind Mapping, Creative Thinking and Problem-Solving, and Meetings.

He was so impressed with the techniques that he spread the training throughout the bank and even included a series of four workshops for the children of employees of the bank. He, and others throughout the bank, have been using the techniques since that time, including software. He writes:

'Project and Quality Management, which is an internal consultancy group at Chase Manhattan Bank in the UK, use Mind-Mapping extensively for helping create new programmes. They manage and coordinate vastly complicated Global projects, such as the recent merger with Chemical Bank and preparations for the introduction of EMU. . . Bankers are not best known for their right brain activities. Mapping on a white board helps us tremendously during brainstorming meetings to develop project plans and our quality initiatives. It significantly improves productivity and team participation. We have more fun and get a far better quality result that everybody buys into.'

CASE STUDY 3

John Shears, of British Telecom, writes:

'As a senior business analyst employed by BT Syncordia Global Solutions (BT's facilities management and outsourcing division), I find that my personal efficiency is enhanced by using Mapping techniques and the MindManager software. Additionally I believe that my company benefits by me using this technique as an aid in focusing on the opportunity and in the design of customized solutions. In designing a facilities management or outsourcing solution one is forced to look at a complex interrelated number of elements such as: customers' business drivers, the culture of the company, commercial viability (for both the customer and BT), geographic reach, human resources, legislation and technical design (often leading edge). Mapping helps firstly to take note of all of the elements in a high level interrelated format, then aids via a process of refinement focus on the total customized solution.

> *'Our team is now taking this process a stage further forward by the intro-duction of a software package (MindManager) that can produce Mind Maps quickly, communicating the information to other team members. I now use the software for my presentations, linking PowerPoint visuals to the overview. It is interesting to note that, using these techniques, the design of a solution is taken well "out of the box" to end up with some very innovative solutions.*
>
> *'All in all I believe that the techniques continually develop lateral thinking for the individual; this can be a very powerful management aid in achieving business targets. I believe that the training BT gave me was money well spent for both BT and my individual development.'*

DELEGATION

Delegation is another of the major challenges that executives face every day. The ability to delegate has been shown to be a critical factor in successful leadership. Using facilitation skills in any meeting, whether it is a group of 50 or one-to-one, creates an emphasis on people working *with* you rather than *for* you. You gain the loyalty of teams and individuals more easily by using facilitation skills in delegation. This means:

- moving from 'telling' to asking and selling ideas;
- allowing others to make suggestions as to how something should be done;
- ensuring each problem or issue is owned; and
- removing the ability for them to blame events on other people.

For example, a manager had been having continuing difficulty with one of her team members who was negative and complaining about one aspect of their strategy. At first, the manager had felt irritated and defensive. She had also taken it upon herself to feel that she personally should solve this problem. However, having learnt more about communication and facili-tation, she allowed the team member to have her say without interruption. Then, instead of feeling that she needed to come up with the solution herself, she asked the team member what she felt should be done and allowed her to take that suggested action. The team member felt validated and put all her energy into remedying the situation. Both the relationship and the performance of the team improved from that time.

ARE YOU A CONTROL FREAK?

There are some people, however, who like to be in control of everything around them. They are often perfectionist and have tendencies towards Type A personalities. They believe their way of doing things is right and find it difficult to accept that other people's way of working might be equally valid. Their style of delegation is to tell people what needs to be done and how to do it. Generally this stifles creativity and growth.

The person who likes to control ends up being overburdened as they never let go enough to allow others to take over the reins occasionally. As people become more secure, assertive and confident, so they become more able to respect the opinion and decisions of those who work with them.

This book is about helping you to manage change positively through self-knowledge. If you have a tendency to control situations, experiment now with letting go and letting others take some of the strain. The added flexibility will allow you to dance more easily on that shifting carpet.

PRESENTATIONS

Presentations are another form of meeting. Once again these need careful planning and preparation. The success-recall process you created in Exercise 7.5 (see page 89, above) helps you to manage any nervousness if you experience anxiety before a presentation. Similarly, the PEP exercise in Exercise 9.7 (see page 120, above) will help you to plan responses before the event. You can use them any time you are nervous before a presentation.

Remember that you have a unique brand and personal contribution to bring to any subject and people enjoy seeing you be yourself. Once again, it is an opportunity to demonstrate your positive energy both within your own company and also to your clients.

Many people claim to be bored in presentations. Why? Presenters often forget that the people in the audience are taking information in through their five senses. Many presentations are just bullet points of written information. The people in the audience want to have their senses stimulated with pictures, sounds and interaction.

The MindManager software can help you to create your presentation structure. You can use it as a visual agenda, hyperlinking graphics and visuals, spreadsheets, charts and Word documents from any branch. This format helps you to remember the content of your presentation more easily and also helps the audience to have strong visual messages to go away with. Reinforce your key messages with powerful visuals so that people can remember the images when they leave the room. Stimulate both sides of your audience's brain. Music with a theme from a movie appropriate to the occasion can work wonders. How about a cake with a message iced on it for everyone to see, taste and enjoy during the refreshment break? This can well be the reminder of the 'sweet taste of success'. Use your imagination to engage your audience's senses!

CASE STUDY 4

The London team of Montana Wines of New Zealand had a need to improve the quality of their sales presentations in order to sell more wine to retail outlets and wine clubs. They had a two-day presentation-skills programme to improve the effectiveness of their wine tastings for prospective customers.

Before the two-day course, they had been delivering presentations that were mainly left-brained and logical, with facts and figures about the wines and the company. They realized these were not effective. The course gave them information about using colour, pictures, stories, memory rhythms and whole-brain communication styles. They came to realize that wine is full of taste and romance and anecdotes and that they could tap into the experiences of those listening to them in order to connect better with their audience.

Afterwards, Richard Wilson, Director of Montana in London, said that the course had 'transformed the way they did business'. The job performance of the participants had 'improved a lot' and their 'subsequent presentations have improved dramatically'. Not only were their presentations more interesting, creative and memorable, but also their meetings at their offices had become faster, more fun and more effective.

Presentations are a two-way communication. As a member of an audience you may forget your personal responsibility to find the material interesting and memorable. As a speaker you may forget that you are having a conversation with your audience, not speaking *at* them. The techniques regarding one-to-one communication that we have included in this chapter are relevant to larger groups too.

TWO-WAY COMMUNICATION: THE EMPTY BUCKET

Communication is about a two-way balance of debit and credit, a system of give and take. If you have continuous debit carried forward day after day, you are going to reach a stage where your overdraft facilities are withdrawn and you end up with an empty bucket, bankrupt of goodwill from the other party involved. Surprisingly enough, this happens more often than you would believe and you are confronted with outbursts that you might have thought uncalled for because you had just not been conscious of the process.

Another way of thinking of this is that each person you are in contact with has a mental score card on which they keep score, with a positive and negative column, which records everything you say to them. At the end of a conversation or a period of time, the columns are mentally added up and you come out with either a plus or a minus score.

Figure 13.1   *The battery*

Examples of debits are the times when people say they will do something and then do not do it, or when someone talks behind people's backs. Credits are when people do a spontaneous act of support or kindness and when someone can be relied on to take necessary action.

EXERCISE 13.3 THE BATTERY

Once you become aware that relating with others is more than mere verbal communication but can result in either draining your energy or recharging you, you can protect yourself. Have you had the experience of being with people who leave you feeling exhausted and yet you continue the relationship with them? We cannot always change this situation, but by becoming aware of it we can prevent our energy being drained by using positive visualization and supportive thinking techniques.

Record here the negative and positive influences in your life:

Negative (eg, 'I feel stupid when I am with John')	Positive (eg, 'Jane helps me to be more creative')

What preventive measures could you take in future? (eg, 'In future I can feel creative and clever when I am with John' and visualize yourself being creative next time you are with John. An alternative would be to avoid being with John too often unless you were feeling strong and confident.)

It can be helpful to identify why one person makes you feel good and another depletes your energy. Use this next exercise to work out why you have positive and negative reactions to certain people.

EXERCISE 13.4 THE EMPTY BUCKET EXERCISE

Think of someone with whom you are aggravated and ask yourself the following:

What is it about this person that aggravates me?

_____

_____

_____

Is it their appearance?

_____

_____

_____

Is it their speech pattern?

_____

_____

_____

Is it what they say?

_____

_____

_____

If it is what they say, do they make derogatory remarks?

_____

_____

_____

Are they negative?

_____

_____

_____

Are they cynical?

_____

_____

_____

Are they critical or judgmental?

_____

_____

_____

Think of someone you like or admire:

_____

_____

_____

Is it their appearance?

_____

_____

_____

Is it their speech pattern?

_____

_____

_____

Is it what they say?

_____

_____

_____

If it is what they say, do they make complimentary remarks?

_____

_____

_____

Are they positive?

_____

_____

_____

Are they enthusiastic?

_____

_____

_____

Are they supportive?

_____

_____

_____

Do they have creative ideas?

_____

_____

_____

From the above, were you able to establish a situation where you were giving more? Or a situation where you were receiving more? If there is someone that you like and they are not reciprocating, it is a warning signal that you need to take remedial action. Boundaries are important – giving of yourself without reciprocity, whether it is in time, support or gifts, can deplete your own energy battery. It is also a symbol of your own value. If you give away too much, there is nothing left.

Be aware, also, that giving can be a form of manipulation, as many people give something with the ulterior motive of asking for something back. So question, when you give something to someone, whether you are giving with the expectation that you wish to receive or whether you are giving for giving's sake.

By being aware of the relationship process, you can bring about balance and harmony and avoid the empty bucket syndrome.

SELF-MANAGEMENT

Your thinking is crucial to the success of your communication. Thinking negatively will register in your body language. Become aware of this and notice if it is counter-productive to your outcome. If so, change it. Negative thoughts and body language often result in conflict. Negative energy is received and will set up negativity in the other person. This is why positive expectations and thoughts are so important to the smooth flowing of communication.

SEVEN STEPS TO DEALING WITH CONFLICT

1. Determine your values and goals. What do you want from the situation? How important is it to you?
2. Keep focused on your positive outcome. Look for a win–win solution.
3. Have positive expectations of a face-to-face encounter: negative thoughts and expectations will be reflected in negative, defensive or aggressive body language. Body language is 58 per cent of a communicated message; voice tone is 35 per cent; and word content a mere 7 per cent.
4. Recognize and acknowledge how you are feeling. If expressing emotions is inappropriate at the time, visualize in your mind's eye packaging them up in wrapping paper and placing them beside you. You can address them at a later stage.
5. Stop and play for time if necessary. Do not be forced into a destructive response by your own compulsion to act or from outside pressure. If you are likely to lose your temper, take time out, or take a few deep breaths and count to 20.
6. If the person you are arguing with is angry, it can be helpful to consider that they would not be angry unless they were in pain. Why are they in pain? Is there something you can do to help them?
7. Later, evaluate the event and decide what you have learned and what you could do differently next time.

There is a story that relates the difference between a warrior and a knight. It is said that a knight will let off arrows in many different directions for a variety of reasons, dissipating his energy. A warrior, on the other hand, waits and only strikes if his life is in mortal danger. It is easy to get wound up in petty conflict and stress at work. Get into the habit of standing back, like the warrior, and preserving your energy for those things you really care about.

OILING THE WHEELS OF THE ENGINE

Incorporating the practices we have described in this chapter will preserve your working relationships, and the smooth running of your meetings.

Few of us live in the same reality. Each person has developed their own view of reality, through their thinking and life experience. The key to good communication is learning to respect and understand the other person's reality. At the same time, maintain your own state of confidence, the ability to express your own needs and opinions and project your brand!

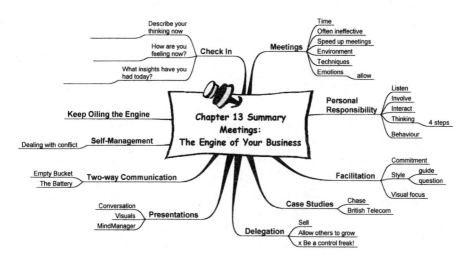

Figure 13.2 *Summary: meetings, the engine of your business*

PART THREE

LOOKING AT THE FUTURE

14

Focusing on the Future

Like any good navigator, you need a good map and a knowledge of your destination. Knowing what you want your brand to be is half the formula to success. The other half is how you get there. Surprisingly few executives can give a detailed description of this. Their outcomes change from day to day depending on a series of variables, eg competition, market conditions, new technology, financial advisers. Obviously you must take into account external variables, but this should not deter you from where you wish to go.

This is where strong inner convictions and a determination to complete your mission come into play. Perhaps you could go back in your life and look at landmark events and ask yourself whether you arrived at them through other people's advice or through your own internal conviction that this was right for you, as we did in Exercise 7.2. Throughout this book you have completed a series of exercises to develop both your intuition and understanding of your thinking, so you can now control your own destiny.

Your brain is like a guided missile and needs a target to give it direction. Provided you supply that target it will find a way to reach it and works 24 hours a day to do so. You also need power and fuel to get lift-off and to maintain velocity on the way. If you are unaware of your own strengths, talents and gifts then that power will be diminished.

There are only so many hours in the day, so how you spend your time will depend on your mission, for the mission gives you the constant criteria on which you can ask yourself the question: 'If I spend my time on this. . . is it helping me to get closer to what I want?' Become *aware* of how you are spending your time and eliminate time-wasters that yield little return. By keeping a daily time log you may discover that on any given day you spend only 15 minutes on an important decision that would take you closer to your mission and five to six hours on 'firefighting' activities.

EXERCISE 14.1 BREAKING THROUGH THE BARRIERS TO MY SUCCESS

Consider the barriers in your own life and in those of your team before you begin the next section to your personal mission statement.

EXERCISE 14.2 UNIQUE VALUE

When you consider what you want your brand to be, you need to consider your own unique value. Your value is derived from the person you are, which emanates from your energy and values, as well as the skills and capabilities you possess.

Figure 14.1 will help you to understand your value. It both focuses on the needs and expectations of others in the marketplace and assists you to appreciate your own unique qualities. Answer the questions on the map as specifically as you can.

Appreciation of your own unique value helps you to communicate that value to those around you. If you have any doubts about your weaknesses in certain areas, reflect upon how you could build them up or view them as positive aspects of yourself. Every person alive has weaknesses and every weakness can be a strength in certain situations and certain perspectives. The more you can be honest with yourself and accept aspects of yourself that may not be perfect, the more you can use them as positive parts of who you are.

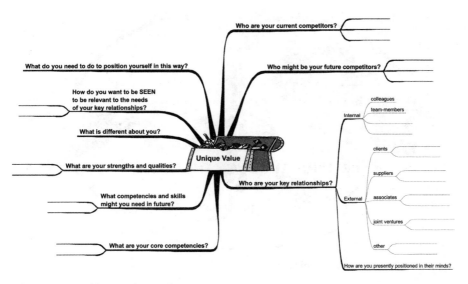

Figure 14.1   *Your unique value*

THE NAVIGATOR: YOUR PERSONAL MISSION STATEMENT

The self-reflection and insights you may have gained through the exercises of the previous chapters can guide you as you design your own mission. If you already have a mission, now is a good chance to review it. You probably now have a clearer idea of what is important to you, what your values are, what you might want for yourself, your department and your organization.

If you need to design a mission, the following exercise will help you.

EXERCISE 14.3 DESIGNING A MISSION

1. Write down the three most important things you personally want to accomplish in the next three years. The one proviso is that this is a win–win for everyone involved. By 'everyone', we mean the people in your company, your family, your community, your clients and your suppliers. Hint: make these a stretch.

1.

_____

_____

_____

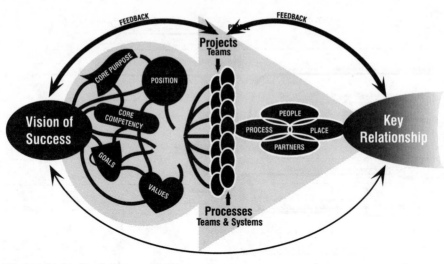

Figure 14.2 *Designing a mission*

2.

_____

_____

_____

3.

_____

_____

_____

Write down the reasons why you wish to accomplish these things.

_____

_____

_____

What difference would they make to your life?

_____

_____

_____

Write down how you will feel once you have accomplished them.

_____

_____

_____

What will people be saying to you?

_____

_____

_____

What picture will be in your mind?

_____

_____

_____

What will you be saying to yourself?

_____

_____

_____

2. Business mission. Now write down the three most important things you want to accomplish within your business. The same proviso applies, that this is a win–win for everyone involved. By 'everyone', we mean the people in your company, your business community, your clients and your suppliers. Hint: make these a stretch.

1.

_____

_____

_____

2.

_____

_____

_____

3.

_____

_____

_____

Write down the reasons why you wish to accomplish these things.

_____

_____

_____

What difference would they make to your life?

_____

_____

_____

Write down how you will feel once you have accomplished them.

_____

_____

_____

What will people be saying to you?

_____

_____

What picture will be in your mind?

_____

_____

_____

What will you be saying to yourself?

_____

_____

_____

Do the above objectives you wrote down in 1 match the objectives you wrote down in 2? If they do, this means that you are in complete alignment in your personal and business missions.

If this is the case, go ahead and develop a personal mission statement. This will act as your guide and compass in future decisions and choices. A mission statement is a short paragraph that sums up your values and brand direction. It is a set of beliefs and principles that are core to your endeavours. When you read it to yourself it needs to strike an emotional chord, a feeling of 'Oh yes! This is what I want. This represents who I want to be.'

An example of a personal mission statement is:

'Living every day true to my values and to myself. Living in love and not in fear, and reflecting this love to those around me. Taking decisions that are true to my core beliefs and being a role model and inspiration for my family, friends and colleagues. Gaining balance in my life, spending time with those I love as well as doing the work I love. Through my work helping others to enjoy a greater quality of life and enabling them to feel powerful enough to reflect their best selves both at home and at work.'

EXERCISE 14.4 PERSONAL MISSION STATEMENT

Your mission statement may be a sentence (hint: as in the example quoted above, always write in the present continuous tense) or a series of bullet points; or a poem, a song, a picture or diagram, or a map or set of key words. Do whatever feels right to you. Develop it with your heart and your mind, allowing yourself to believe you will achieve it. You can write or design it in the space overleaf.

ALIGNMENT

If there is little or no match between your present personal and organizational mission, it means you may be compromising either yourself or the corporation. Making personal compromises can deplete your energy levels and even lead to illness. Compromises at work are likely to deplete the energy levels of those around you (see Exercise 13.3, page 182, above). This will affect the overall performance of the team, both in terms of communication and results.

ORGANIZATIONAL MISSION STATEMENT

If it is an organizational or departmental mission you are creating, then you need to consult with your team. By forcing your views of mission and purpose, others may resent it and not feel valued. Have you seen corporate reception areas where mission statements hang on the wall, paying lip service to a set of values that others feel indifferent to and may not even understand? An effective mission statement will reflect a synthesis of the thinking of all those involved. It will excite, and motivate them to action, acting as a navigational compass to decision-making.

A mission statement is a catalyst for change. It symbolizes the moving from one point to another. Other people may need help in preparing for this change. If you are the sponsor of this activity then it is helpful to realize that they may not be as ready as you are to move on. They may need to express their feelings about the present situation before they are able to take this next step.

It is advisable to have an external consultant assist you in this process. This creates a safe environment for people to express themselves without fear of comeback. Through good facilitation you should be able to reach a mission statement which all present agree to and buy into.

EXAMPLES OF ORGANIZATIONAL MISSION STATEMENTS

'To help our Clients change to be more successful.' (Andersen Consulting)

'We shall work with our customers to deliver superior products and services, making it easier for anyone to harness the power of personal computing to their best advantage.' (Microsoft)

'Company Principle: Maintaining an international viewpoint, we are dedicated to supplying products of the highest efficiency at a reasonable price for worldwide customer satisfaction. Management Policy: Proceed always with ambition and youthfulness. Respect sound theory, develop fresh ideas and make the most effective use of time. Enjoy your work and always brighten your working atmosphere. Strive constantly for a harmonious flow of work. Be ever mindful of the value of research and endeavour.' (Honda Motor Company)

'We believe our first responsibility is to the doctors, nurses and patients, to mothers and fathers and all others who use our products and services. . . We are responsible to the communities in which we live and work and to the world community as well. We must be good citizens – support good works and charities and bear our fair share of taxes. We must encourage civic improvements and better health and education. We must maintain in good order the property we are privileged to use, protecting the environment and natural resources.' (Johnson & Johnson)

EXERCISE 14.5 RECORD YOUR ORGANIZATIONAL MISSION STATEMENT

If you have an organizational mission statement, record it here. Otherwise, write it down when you have developed it with your team.

_____

_____

_____

_____

_____

_____

_____

_____

Both personal and organizational missions need to be reviewed and updated as you and your team are changing on a daily basis. A mission represents a desirable place to reach on your continuous journey. Once you arrive, you need to celebrate and decide what's next.

MAKING IT HAPPEN

You know from the previous study of your brain that each time you repeat a thought it builds up a chemical pathway that develops a thinking and behavioural habit. When setting goals in place, it is also necessary that you build up a visual and multi-sensory image of what you wish to achieve. Input from the eye goes immediately into the limbic part of our brain, which controls our emotional response. It then transmits the information to the upper cortical thinking area. However, the first impact is emotional.

This is why visualization itself is so powerful in changing your state and in helping you to change behaviour. The messages from your eye, or your constructed image, will release associated endorphins, hormones and energy and give your body and mind a pleasurable sensation that can help to motivate you in the achievement of your goal.

In order to start using more of our brain power than the logical/linguistic intelligence encompasses, we need to develop a technology which utilizes all of the 12 intelligences mentioned in Chapter 8. We are now in a position to develop a whole new mental technology known as inner modelling. This next exercise is one of the most powerful ways of helping you to manage yourself in both the present and the future. You may wish to tape-record the next instructions or have a friend read them to you.

EXERCISE 14.6 THE INNER MODELLING PROCESS

Find a time when, and a place where, you will not be interrupted. Either lying down flat or seated with your back straight, take a few deep breaths which will relax you and take you into an alpha state (see Exercise 9.5 on page 118 for guidance on how to reach an alpha state). In your mind's eye, see a picture of your mission accomplished three years from now. Once you have established this picture, ensure that the following components are installed:

- The picture is in colour.
- The picture is in a frame.

- You are in the picture.
- You play a favourite uplifting piece of music mentally each time you look at that picture.
- You have good feelings when you are in this coloured picture of yourself in the frame with the music.
- As well as the music soundtrack, you hear familiar voices congratulating you as you progress along the path of your mission and reach desired goals.
- When you have established this picture and the soundtrack, clench a fist to anchor the experience with physical tension. Note that each time you pull up this picture and soundtrack you should at the same time clench your fist. The repetition of this strengthens the whole process in your long-term memory.
- Now that you are picturing yourself in the future successfully living your mission, mentally look back over the last three years to the present time as if you were reviewing a movie. As you view your movie and go through the time frame of 36 months, notice how obstacles arose and how you overcame them; notice your anchor and how the strong positive emotional feeling used assisted you through difficult times. At the end of the exercise take a deep breath, and come back to the present.

We strongly recommend that you do this each evening before retiring.

You may capture this on paper so that you have a record of both the obstacles you may face and the techniques you used to overcome them.

The above technique is how many future Olympic athletes around the world are currently being trained by their professional psychological coaches for future victories. Now you have the opportunity to use the same mental technique as top athletes to become one of the world's outstanding business people.

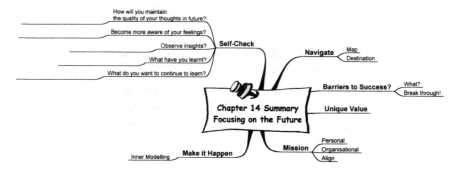

Figure 14.3 *Summary: focusing on the future*

Have you considered that imagination, used both positively and negatively, is stronger than willpower? This simple truth has enormous consequences for the way we conduct our daily business lives. It means that simply working long and hard does not necessarily guarantee success, whereas using your imagination in the way we have outlined above can reap rapid rewards.

Now you understand how important it is to look daily at your mission's attractive future. This way you are reinforcing the mental image, the message, the values and the feelings that are so important to you. You are, in other words, applying your brain's success mechanism to create your own success.

15

The Road Ahead

In Chapter 14, 'Focusing on the Future', you set a three-year timeframe to achieve your mission. As time goes by, you will be updating this mission and pushing out a further three years ahead into the future. Even though shareholders might demand short-term returns, your career path is a much longer journey, requiring stamina, physical and mental fitness, and agility. For you personally it is a continuous journey and, whilst staying true to the values and principles of your mission, you need to remain flexible and creative as circumstances present themselves.

Imagine yourself as a building, with your values, beliefs and mission as your foundations and structure. Think then of the storms or earthquakes that might buffet you and remember that it is the buildings with strong foundations but flexibility that can adapt to the environment, that keep standing in an earthquake, just as the tree with a flexible trunk will survive a hurricane. The more mentally fit you are, the more adaptable you are to change. Also, by being physically fit, you will have the strength and energy needed to keep dancing on that shifting carpet.

Any journey starts with a single step. Each morning, take time to consider what needs to be done that day and how you might do it. Focus on how you would like to feel that day and what emotional state will support you in the actions you need to take. Use your memory and imagination to draw in that feeling.

Question your methods; develop new ways of thinking, new paradigms of life. It may feel uncomfortable at first, but remember that if it does not feel uncomfortable then it is unlikely that you are changing or doing things differently. The discomfort is a clue to the fact that you are, indeed, adopting new ways of doing things, new ways of seeing life. It can be extraordinarily exciting and can add zest to every activity, both at work and at home. The following exercises are designed to help you expand your thinking and behaviour.

EXERCISE 15.1 CREATIVE ADVENTURES

Do something different every day:

- change your morning routine;
- wear a different outfit;
- eat different food for breakfast;
- go to work by a different route;
- treat your colleagues differently;
- change your office layout;
- bring colour into your thinking at work;
- go somewhere new for lunch;
- talk to a member of staff you have rarely spoken to before;
- think of something your colleagues do not yet know about you and share it;
- think about a new client base you may not have considered before;
- look at your products or services and think up some zany new ideas;
- think of a new and fun activity for teambuilding;
- get home on time to play a silly game with your children;
- be a little more frivolous than usual;
- buy something unusual to eat;
- treat your partner to something romantic and different;
- watch the sunset;
- look at the world afresh and from a new perspective;
- bathe, shower or wash with your eyes closed;
- clean your teeth with your other hand;
- skip a meal;
- watch television with the sound off.

Try any or all of these, and more of your own, and write down your experiences. Observe your colleagues and question whether you might be able to inspire them to think creatively.

'*No problem can be solved from the same consciousness that created it. We must learn to see the world anew.' (Albert Einstein)*

EXERCISE 15.2 STEP ONE: MAKING A DIFFERENCE

- Develop crazy ideas about how you will reach your goals.
- What ideas can you have to ensure you do *not* reach your goal?
- What ideas might get you sacked?
- Look at your competitors and see if you get any ideas from what they are doing.
- If you were a clown, what might you do differently?
- If you were a small child, what might you do differently?
- Look around the corner at yourself and give yourself a piece of advice that you might not have thought about yet.
- Think of the most successful person you know and consider what advice they might give you.
- If you were a person from another country, how might you tackle these steps differently?
- If you only had a few days to live, how might you decide the fastest way to live your mission?
- If you were starting your life all over again, what might you do now to ensure that you live your mission?

From some of these seemingly ridiculous exercises you will be able to draw out some themes that will help you develop creative ways of thinking and behaving. You can also use these questions in brainstorming sessions with your team in order to inspire new ways of thinking.

DECISIONS

Decision-making is not always straightforward, due to the complexity of the decision, the people involved and the emotions that come into play.

Question how open you are to the views and input of others and how much you involve them in your decision-making processes. Are you nervous of opposition so you make decisions alone? If you avoid conflict at the outset, you may find you experience resentment later when others discover they have not been involved in the decision.

Many managers do not understand the power of asking for the views of their team in making a decision. This can lead to over-control and to one-dimensional thinking and decision-making. Such managers can find themselves accused of manipulation if, for example, they have decided upon what they consider the best course of action before they hold a meeting.

FOLLOW-UP

Working with leaders and executive teams around the world, we have observed that, despite having excellent mission statements, marketing strategies and plans, many of these fall down in the area of follow-up. Follow-up is a key factor to success. Projects and initiatives that are not sustained cost organizations countless sums of money.

So why is this follow-up so critically important? Studies of the human brain show that information that is not reinforced by review and/or follow-up within 24 hours has an 80 per cent evaporation rate. Consider these implications with regard to meetings where minutes are not rapidly circulated; training programmes where millions of pounds are spent daily with no review; marketing programmes where nothing happens for weeks after the launch. All of this initial effort, resource and money is in many cases totally wasted simply because the respondents forget what it is all about. Therefore it is critical to understand Figure 15.1, which illustrates memory rhythms.

Figure 15.1 illustrates the importance of following up not only externally with projects and training but also with your own internal agendas. Repetition is the key to learning. When you are making changes in your behaviour you are undertaking a learning activity: you are learning new ways of thinking, learning and communicating. This learning needs to be reinforced daily, if possible several times a day, for change to take place.

When you review, use your whole sensory system and your whole brain: review logically and rationally what changes you want to make. You can do this by reading aloud to yourself so that you both see and hear the message or make a tape and play it in your car as you drive to work.

EXERCISE 15.3 MAKING SURE IT HAPPENS

Here are some suggestions to help you reinforce change:

- make lists and plans of how you will organize yourself, your team, your projects;

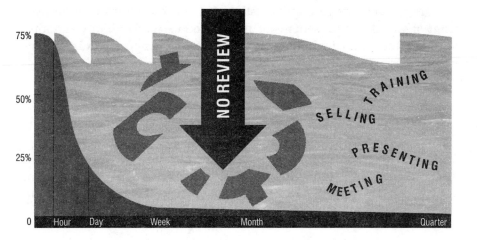

Figure 15.1 *Learning review*

- put a visual memory trigger on or near your desk (a map or Post-It note of your goals or a symbol that will remind you of new behaviours);
- consider the number of steps involved;
- make diary entries to keep you focused, using the journal at the back of this book;
- picture yourself making these steps and arriving at your successful outcome;
- feel it and hear the difference both in your internal thinking and in what others might be saying to you;
- see the big picture and also see the small chunks that it takes to get there.

Complete your personal commitment to change by noting down how you will remember to do things differently in future:

_____

_____

_____

You have now moved from the big picture to the details that get work done. You are designing your own roadmap to the future. As any notable artist will tell you, they always start with the big picture in mind, then fill in their canvas with an array of paints, techniques and splashes of creative genius.

You are the artist of your own destiny and you have this blank canvas in front of you that represents your future. You can now fill in your canvas with the tools and techniques of this book to support your successful outcome.

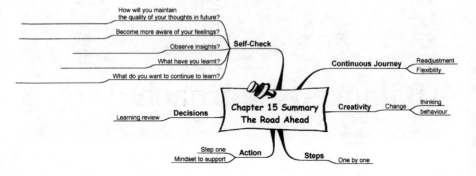

Figure 15.2 *Summary: the road ahead*

16

A Balanced Approach

By now you are likely to have begun to understand yourself better and made some decisions as to changes you wish to introduce into your life. The emphasis of this book is your path to success at work through this self-knowledge.

However, you do not operate in a vacuum at work. You take to work the same body, emotions and thoughts that you have experienced outside the workplace. If you are experiencing problems outside work, then they will impact upon how you approach your daily tasks and also on how you communicate with your colleagues and clients.

If, for example, you are not eating a healthy diet at home then you will be experiencing a lack of energy and well-being at work. If your worries are preventing you from sleeping well then you will drag an over-tired mind into your meetings and decisions at work. If you are feeling guilty that you are not giving enough time to your family and friends, that guilt will impact upon your stress levels and be a nagging voice in your head at times when your thinking needs to be focused clearly on the matters of the day. If you are experiencing conflict with your partner then you are likely to be experiencing heightened emotions that may affect your behaviour in general. Your car may have broken down; your dishwasher may need to be mended and yet you are feeling you cannot spare the time to wait in for the service engineer.

As Leonardo da Vinci once said, 'Everything connects to everything else', so it is important for you to use the insights you have gained so far to reassess and make changes in all areas of your life, not just at work.

So often in the work we do within organizations, we find a culture that emphasizes all work and no play. This tends to emanate from the leaders and executives of that business. Long-hours culture can result in anything from stress to nervous breakdowns, illness, burnout, disruption of the family unit and numerous other problematic situations. The emphasis on immediate bottom-line results is putting pressure on people in work to perform at ever higher levels.

In a new survey, 'Enabling Balance: The Importance of Organizational Culture', by the Roffey Park Management Institute in the UK, it is reported that almost 70 per cent of managers are suffering from increased levels of stress due to rising workloads. A staggering 96 per cent agree that extra working hours are expected of a manager today, and 94 per cent claim that their companies do not provide support to remedy this matter. The National Work-Life Forum reports that stress is a major cause of absenteeism and lost productivity in the UK. A company of 1,000 employees can expect around 2–300 of its staff to suffer from anxiety-related illnesses each year. Inevitably this is affecting bottom-line performance (*Director* magazine, June 1999).

There are immediate techniques to achieve a balance of life through the development of thinking systems and practices within organizations. In the meantime, however, most staff adopt the working practices of senior management and therefore work harder and harder and for longer and longer periods of time, neglecting other areas of their lives.

We experienced a case recently where a senior executive was under so much pressure to achieve his targets that he was often working literally 24 hours a day, taking a cat-nap occasionally but unable to put his targets into perspective. His health suffered: he experienced bad headaches, skin disorders, loss of energy, and irritability. His diet suffered: he ordered in take-away pizzas, hamburgers and chips and ate very little fresh food. He did not allow himself time to go to the gym and take exercise. He had no time for his friends. He read little, talked to few people. In fact, anything that was not directly focused on the achievement of his target was neglected. His perspective had become unbalanced; he therefore had little lateral or broad-scope information to bring to his approach to work or to his decisions. His team were losing patience and not responding well to his attempts to inspire cooperation.

It took only four sessions of coaching to turn many of these problems around. And that was simply by helping him to hold a mental mirror up to himself so that he could reflect on how he was living his life, and on how the imbalance in his own life was impacting on his team at work. With a few simple but practical thinking tools, models and questions, he was able to change his thinking and behaviour, his routine and the way he communicated with his staff. Within a week his skin disorder had disappeared; by the fourth session he was sleeping well, not working all weekend, and planning his sessions at the gym. His team, who had previously taken a 'nine to five' attitude, volunteered enthusiastically to work late to help him achieve a deadline. They said they saw and felt the difference in him and it changed the way they responded to him.

THE TREADMILL

This is only one example of how your whole life affects your work. It is also only one example in a world where there are thousands of people living the same kind of life as this senior executive. It is an illustration of how senior managers can help both themselves and those with whom they work to ensure that these imbalances do not occur.

Figure 16.1

However, if the senior management of your organization is not setting an example in this area then you can take personal responsibility for bringing balance into your own life. Work in the United States by Dean Ornish (see Chapter 9 above) proves that rest, relaxation, meditation and healthy personal relationships are critical to your well-being. What happens within organizations influences thousands of other people – friends, families, communities and, perhaps most importantly, the children who observe and experience these practices, where work becomes the all-encompassing driver of people's lives. Is this the role model you wish to hand down to them?

Despite the statistics that demonstrate that people are working ever harder, most of the senior executives we speak to individually agree that this is a crazy lifestyle. They realize that these pressures put people at work in danger of ending up with a very narrow focus and little information about other industries, other countries, other factors of life that can help to give them a broader perspective on life. It is unlikely that they will be able to make good decisions without a reasonable knowledge and understanding of other areas.

Many tell us that they would rather work from home; that they spend so long at work that they seldom give time to the other areas of life that are important to them. They also know that it is not an effective way to use either their brain or their body's energy – neither of which can be expected to remain alert for 13 hours a day without time for refreshment.

Why, then, is it so difficult for these senior individuals who influence working practices to address these problems? Could it be that if these individuals opened up to communicate to colleagues in a more honest way they would come to realize how many other people are similarly worried about this situation? With this sharing and support, perhaps they would come to realize that these demands are affecting the whole of society in a radical way. Divorce rates are going up as a result of these pressures; young people in work have too little time or energy at the end of the day to create relationships; surveys relate couples playing the 'I'm more tired than you are' game in order to avoid household chores.

Work practices in organizations have never been more influential as more and more men and women work either full time or part time under their aegis. With unemployment high, some companies make extraordinary demands on their staff in the knowledge that those staff may perceive that they have little choice but to accept whatever is handed down to them. One could draw some similarities to the Industrial Revolution and to the legislation that had to be introduced at that time to prevent the worst excesses of this power structure. Despite the flattening of organizational structures, these excesses continue, and it is for this reason that governments are introducing new 'family-friendly' legislation today to curb these imbalances.

As you read and consider this, is there anything that you personally are doing or could do to prevent these imbalances growing worse for future generations? To start this process of thinking, begin with your own life and look at the demands you face personally on a daily basis:

EXERCISE 16.1 ROLES AND RESPONSIBILITIES

1. List your various roles and responsibilities at work (for example, CEO, senior manager, manager, team leader, colleague, boss, direct report, client-liaison, marketing, administration, filing, computer operation, telephone communicator, financial responsibilities, etc). List on a scale of 1–10 their importance in helping you to achieve the mission and goals you have listed in the previous chapters; list also your level of enjoyment.

	Role	Responsibility (mark out of 10)	Goal-orientation (mark out of 10)	Enjoyment	Conflict with other roles
Eg	Team leader	success of team	9/10	7/10	8/10
1.					
2.					
3.					
4.					
5.					
6.					
7.					
8.					
9.					
10.					

2. List your various roles and responsibilities at home (for example, partner, parent, brother, sister, daughter, son, friend, planning, financial responsibilities, sport, relaxation, theatre, film, hobbies, restaurants, social, time alone, pet-walker, pet-feeder, gardening, housekeeping, etc).

	Role	Responsibility (mark out of 10)	Goal-orientation (mark out of 10)	Enjoyment	Conflict with other roles
Eg	Father	share parenting	10/10	9/10	9/10
1.					
2.					
3.					
4.					
5.					
6.					
7.					
8.					
9.					
10.					

3. Now write any comments, goals or conclusions you may have as a result of doing that exercise:

_____

_____

_____

_____

_____

_____

You have a multitude of roles that you play daily and the appreciation of the diversity of these roles can help you to develop more lateral ways of thinking about your talents and capabilities. Many people who have been made redundant or who have faced career changes in their lives have used the broader view of their activities to identify their transferable skills. It also helps you decide how you wish to divide your time in future.

EXERCISE 16.2 THE LIFE QUOTIENT

Taking the whole of your life as 100 per cent, divide the following activities into this figure and decide what percentage of your time you wish to give to each activity:

- Work
- Family
- Friends
- Spirituality
- Sports
- Health clubs
- Food and diet
- Leisure time
- Civic duties
- Self development
- Recreational travel
- Business travel
- Other

Inevitably, life changes from day to day so it may not always be possible to adhere to these divisions. They act as a guideline and need not be rigid. However, they give your brain a focus and another vision of success to help you to gain quality of life.

DIET

The type of food you eat has a direct influence on the performance of your brain. If you are eating stodgy foods your brain will function less well. The brain takes 25 per cent of the body's energy reserves. If the body is busy digesting bulky food, this will affect the ability of your mind to think clearly.

This needs to be considered at business functions and lunches if you are to communicate information and/or make serious decisions after participating in a meal. Many conferences, meetings and seminars are punctuated with large and over-rich meals. This is unlikely to stimulate creative thinking if provided at lunchtime.

A common habit in offices is to consume endless cups of tea and coffee. Whilst coffee can, in moderation, stimulate thinking, creativity and memory, if taken to excess it can induce palpitations, sweating and anxiety. If taken towards the end of the day it can cause insomnia. Like alcohol, it is addictive, and so if you notice that you are drinking several cups of coffee a day you could try to exchange a caffeinated coffee for a decaffeinated coffee and see if you notice any changes.

The healthiest drink of all is fresh water. As your body is made up of a large percentage of water, you need to replenish its stocks. Health groups advise that we should ideally drink 1–2 litres of fresh water – preferably not sparkling – per day. It is good for the kidneys, blood and therefore the brain. It is also regarded as one of the most effective ways of losing weight.

Fresh fruit and vegetables are, by their very nature, sources of energy. They are rich in nutrients and are quickly and easily digested. In the UK the Government has recently been promoting the benefits of eating five servings of fruit and vegetables per day. These are seen to play a part in preventing cancer, as well as in providing vital energy.

Fish contain ingredients that actively develop the nutrients necessary for the brain. Meat is also a source of protein, which gives you energy. A high-protein meal can increase mental alertness. How we think is, therefore, directly influenced by what we eat.

Many people are beginning to take zinc and iron supplements with their diet, and this is because we are becoming aware that the 'healthy diet' of less red meat, more vegetables and white meat is deficient in these elements. A lack of zinc and iron reduces the body's immune system and may temporarily lower mental capabilities. Vitamin B6 is another ingredient necessary in the brain's synthesis of neurotransmitters. It can be found in meat and eggs.

Men and women need to understand that their food requirements may well be different. Balance is an individual decision. Each of us has different chemistries and different tastes. Guilt over adhering, or not, to a diet can cause stress and therefore, in itself, be detrimental to health. Enjoyment is the greatest source of well-being a human being can access. Finding a way to enjoy your diet and feel good about what you eat will enhance both your brain performance and your well-being.

EXERCISE 16.3 DIET MONITOR

Consider the quality of the food you are eating on a regular basis.

List typical meals:

_____

_____

_____

Consider the enjoyment level you associate with these meals:

_____

_____

_____

Reflect and observe how certain foods affect your energy:

_____

_____

_____

What changes might you make?

_____

_____

_____

PHYSIOLOGY

The quality of your breathing is fundamental to clarity of thinking. As the brain takes up 25 per cent of oxygen from your body, then it clearly gets this supply from the quality of your breathing. Few of us are taught how to breathe effectively from our diaphragm. Shallow breathing in the upper respiratory tract is not an efficient way of circulating oxygen through the body. In fact shallow breathing, which often occurs as a result of stress, only increases a nervous state.

Become more aware of how you are breathing and begin to learn to breathe more deeply from your diaphragm. Once you have begun to make this more of a habit, you will find that your energy level rises. If you have a difficult situation to face, take a couple of deep breaths: it can clear your thinking and calm your nerves.

EXERCISE 16.4 DIAPHRAGM BREATHING

To breathe into the diaphragm, straighten the spine and take in a deep breath. Imagine the breath as if it were water being poured into a large balloon, running into the deepest part of your diaphragm and extending it, like a balloon that is full of water. Hold the breath for a count of 2–3 seconds and then slowly release the breath through your mouth. Feel the 'balloon' deflate.

Practise this two or three times a day, particularly on waking up in the morning, to clear your system, and just before retiring to bed, to relax you before sleep. If you find yourself stressed in a meeting, it is very simple to take a couple of seconds to breathe and centre your thoughts inward before carrying on. Keep a watch on your tension level. If you feel tension in your neck and shoulders, or find yourself clenching your jaw or fists at work, this type of breathing can be very effective in easing this physiological tension.

EXERCISE

The effects of exercise on the performance of the brain are radical. As the brain is greedy for oxygen, spending long periods of your day sitting at a desk will be depriving it of oxygen. It is essential, therefore, to ensure that you move around your office and give yourself a break from sitting at least once every hour. Just a few minutes of walking around your office, or walking down the corridor, will help. Fresh air is revitalizing in itself. Finding time to walk in the park or in a beauty spot can refresh both mind and body.

In addition to this, taking good physical exercise two or three times a week will help to give your brain the oxygen it needs. It is preferable if this exercise can include some type of aerobic activity such as fast walking, jogging, running, playing tennis, squash, football, swimming, etc. Choose to walk to a bus or train, to walk to the shops rather than take the car, take the stairs rather than the elevator. Stretching activities such as Yoga and Tai Chi are also effective in building up a strong and healthy body.

It is easy, if you have a busy schedule, to decide that you do not have time to fit exercise into your routine. It is also easy to imagine that if you cannot undertake at least one hour's exercise it is not worth undertaking any. However, you will find that the discipline of participating in some form of exercise, even if it is only 5, 10, or 40 minutes each day or every other day, will pay handsome dividends. The more energy you generate by doing this type of activity, the more energy you will have for every other aspect of your life. Strengthening your body also strengthens your sense of self-confidence and power in general. It is these small daily disciplines that build self-esteem. With each small activity that is achieved, you reinforce the feeling of control you have in your life.

ENVIRONMENT

A pleasing environment is uplifting at work as well as at home. Small changes can make a difference to the way you think and to your motivation level: a plant, a picture, something colourful to stimulate your right cortex and that gives you pleasure when you look at it.

Clutter around you can clutter your mind. Clear space around you. Take time out to go through any piles of papers, magazines and journals in your office and analyse what you need to read and keep and what can be thrown away. If the eye is an emotional trigger zone, then each time you look at the files or papers you need to deal with you will be causing yourself stress. This activity is likely only to take an hour or so of your time but will clear the decks and enable you to identify priorities.

Clarity of thinking is much simpler if you have an orderly desk and filing systems. It is easy to procrastinate about this type of repetitive administrative work but the rewards are noticeable not only in terms of physical space but also in terms of your thinking and emotion when you look at that space.

If you have trouble motivating yourself to do this type of work, and are unable to delegate it, help yourself by thinking how good it will feel when you are finished. Rather than seeing the job as one that you have to plough through, take your mind to the end-result and feel the satisfaction you will experience. This will motivate you to move ahead. And, of course, always reward yourself when you have achieved the desired result, or even a step towards it.

We now have more information than ever on how to live a healthy balanced life. With the knowledge explosion you are now living through, there is no question that this whole area will reveal many more secrets in the years to come. You are strongly recommended to keep up to date in an area vital to your business performance, your health, happiness, and longevity.

A study in the UK recently estimated that those born after the year 1943 have a 50 per cent likelihood of living until they are 100. This has a radical impact on how you plan your future in terms of health, finance and career. Maintaining a balanced and healthy lifestyle gives you a better chance of remaining fit, energetic and able to keep earning for as long as you may require.

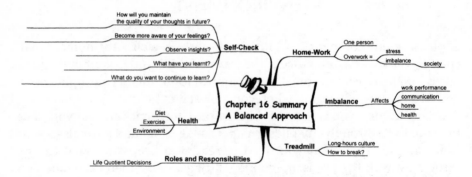

Figure 16.2   *Summary: a balanced approach*

17

The Sense of Self

In this book we have brought you up to date with the latest research on the brain, and on human behaviour, so that you may benefit in a practical way from what is now the last frontier, the human mind. More specifically, we have endeavoured to give you the opportunity to take time to hold a mirror up to your own mind and determine what part your thinking is playing in the situations you are manifesting and experiencing at work. This process is to enable you to develop a sense of yourself and your own unique value, or 'brand'.

You may be wondering what this all means to you and may be a little overwhelmed by what you may consider to be a daunting amount of change that needs to occur in your life. On the other hand, you may well already be incorporating many of the principles outlined in this book into your current behaviour. Whatever your present position, the achievement of your goals will come from a step-by-step approach.

Here are some suggestions for how you may wish to proceed from here.

EXERCISE 17.1 CHECKING IN

Take your Thirty-day Planner, which appears in Appendix 1 to this book. For the next 30 days use the journal three times a day, for example at the hours of 10 am, 1 pm and 4 pm. When those times arrive, briefly make a note in your diary in the following areas:

1. What is the quality of your thoughts at that moment?
2. What are you feeling at that moment?
3. What is your state of awareness? This could mean being 100 per cent focused on the present, and not drifting off into the past, or into the future.

Regard this as the methodology to adopt new and healthy habits, not as a chore. Not only does this cover the built-in 24-hour memory rhythm, but it also acts as a feedback loop on your progress and as a reminder to reward yourself when you are successful. This means doing something nice for yourself such as treating yourself to something you personally want to do, be it a visit to the gym, having a massage, buying a new pair of shoes, or having an evening out.

Often the role of leadership can be a lonely one. Many of the senior executives we work with admit to feeling isolated. Whatever your role, we strongly recommend that you do not fall into this mode. Go out of your way to build a support group. This group does not necessarily need to be people in the same industry but can be made up of varied individuals whom you trust and respect and who are accessible to you.

EXERCISE 17.2 SUPPORT NETWORK

1. Think of five people who can form part of your support group, and list their names below with address, fax, telephone and e-mail numbers.

1.

_____

_____

_____

2.

_____

_____

_____

3.

_____

_____

_____

4.

_____

_____

_____

5.

_____

_____

_____

2. Contact them and ask them, in whatever way feels appropriate to you, if they would be kind enough to be part of your support group. This may mean meeting with them regularly in person over lunch or in the evenings, over a golf match or a game of cards. Alternatively, you can develop a support relationship by phone or e-mail.

3. Allow the relationship to develop in a way where you can talk about your current daily activities with regard both to your trials and to your triumphs. Be prepared to do the same for them. Give one another recognition and appreciation so as to ensure it is a mutually rewarding experience. How you do this will vary from country to country and from culture to culture.

An alternative to a support group is a personal coach. There is now a whole new movement of personal coaches: people whom you may never meet but just speak to on the phone on a regular basis and who help you through your daily business routine. These coaches are trained facilitators and you may find a lot of help and comfort in having someone who is a skilled listener and can ask you important questions to reveal your thoughts and feelings on key issues.

A good deal of success begins by simply acting the role. Consider how you could do this. We are not suggesting you take on another personality: simply take on the characteristics you would most like to adopt, as this allows you to begin to reflect your best attributes to others. Observe those around you and notice what you admire. One sometimes hears people express jealousy at another person's clothing or attributes. Instead of focusing on jealousy, try to consider whether you could mimic what they are doing – not precisely, but in your own way. It does not always take a large investment of money to adopt the habits and trimmings of your desired lifestyle.

EXERCISE 17.3 YOUR BEST SELF-VISUALIZATION

Take five minutes now to close your eyes and build up a multi-sensory image of the achievement of your goals.

Details make the difference. Try to surround yourself as much as possible with the things that please you and the people who support you.

Treat yourself to a quality lifestyle and this will be reflected in who you are, how you behave and in the way others treat you. It is about valuing yourself and committing yourself to the future you desire.

In your mind's eye, feel that you are now the person you want to become. Consider how you would react, and how others would be reacting to you. Feel strong and powerful within that scene.

It can help to look forward to your ideal future scenario and to the type of person you wish to become. Think about what activities you will be undertaking, where you would like to be, what financial rewards you would like to be enjoying, how you will feel; and then base your decisions as single-mindedly as you can on that outcome.

Take five minutes to do this now.

Think of a word that will remind you of this feeling on a daily basis:

_____

_____

_____

Today more than ever you have to be your own PR consultant. You may well change your career many times during your lifetime. Your image and your own personal 'branding' are therefore crucially important. How you 'write yourself up', either on paper or orally, sends signals to others about your sense of personal value.

To continue to feel and be successful in this ever-changing world demands that you yourself know and appreciate what your value is. If you do not know, then it is certainly less likely that others will notice. When you know more about who you are, you will know where you are going, why, and how you are going to get there. A management consultant remarked recently that he would not advise a client to do business with someone who lacked self-knowledge because they may not understand why they are entering that contract and therefore may not be committed to its success. Self-knowledge brings that clarity.

With this self-knowledge comes the development of your multi-intelligence. Your chances of success grow as you learn to use more of the multiple intelligences we discussed in Chapter 8. Add to this the ability to be emotionally intelligent and to continue to manage yourself in the midst of pressure and you will truly be able to dance on that shifting carpet. In a recent study to identify the overall predictors of management success, carried out by the Henley Management College and published in the *Training Journal* in June 1999, it was found that:

- 27 per cent of the variance of success was predicted by IQ;
- 16 per cent was predicted by other management competencies; and
- 36 per cent was predicted by the emotional competencies.

It is therefore your ability to harness a combination of all your talents, qualities and capabilities that gives you personal resilience and the ability to motivate yourself to perform at your best, even in difficult circumstances. And there will always be ups and downs in life.

Each day your value grows. Each day you learn new things, and once an insight is gained it is always there, stored in your knowledge bank. It is your responsibility to maximize that potential; no one will do it for you!

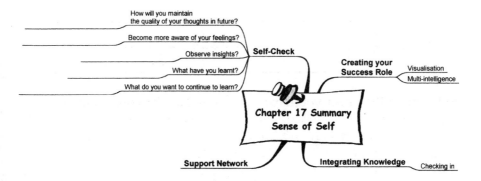

Figure 17.1 *Summary: sense of self*

You do not have to be a prisoner of your past mistakes or experiences. You can break free now to focus on and develop all your stronger attributes.

The journey to self-knowledge is a continuous one: stop and appreciate each goal as you achieve it and yet keep your mind alert to the fact that as your life changes so do you. It is a progressive and exciting journey of revelation that reaps infinite rewards in all areas of your life.

In this way you can live every day as if you are living out your own success story. We believe and hope that this book will help you to do so.

Appendix 1

Thirty-Day Planner

Fifty activities to keep your brain and body healthy. Read these and enter some into your journal for the next 30 days:

1. Think positive, quality thoughts.
2. Eat healthy foods and a balanced diet.
3. Have ample rest every day.
4. Daydream every day.
5. Associate with inspiring business people.
6. Avoid office gossip.
7. Focus on what you have, and not on what you do not have.
8. Exercise on a regular basis.
9. Take mini-breaks throughout the day.
10. Spend time each day in meditation, no matter how short.
11. Visualize how you want to live your life.
12. Have a regular medical check-up.
13. Keep your inner voice supportive to your goals.
14. Establish a calm manner throughout the business day.
15. Put your business goals in writing and keep them where you can see them daily.
16. Review and update your business goals on a regular basis.
17. Listen to inspiring music.

18. Read quality business materials, newspapers and magazines.
19. Spend ample time with family and friends.
20. Take annual vacations.
21. Drink eight glasses of water every day.
22. Have hobbies and interests outside of your normal work.
23. Live a balanced life.
24. Cultivate a new interest each year.
25. Attend lectures on interesting subjects.
26. Keep a daily diary.
27. Think about what you are going to say before you say it.
28. Become more aware of your emotions.
29. Express your emotions whenever appropriate.
30. Learn to express appreciation at work whenever you can.
31. Make eye contact with other people, and be friendly.
32. Think of ways you can be of service to your fellow workers.
33. Communicate freely and do not withhold information.
34. Learn to say 'thank you'.
35. Work at improving your memory.
36. Walk with purpose and rhythm.
37. Be honest with yourself and others.
38. Be reliable and keep appointments.
39. Take responsibility for your work, life and actions.
40. Learn to be an excellent listener.
41. Learn to love yourself and not be concerned with what others might think of you.
42. Be conscious of your breathing and how it can calm you.
43. Be your own person and do not be too dependent on others.
44. Be grateful for all you have in your life.
45. Do something different and creative once a week.
46. Develop your multiple intelligences.
47. Observe and become sensitive to other people's communication style.
48. Go into meetings with positive expectations.
49. Walk tall, straighten your spine, open your lungs, relax your neck and shoulders.
50. Change your thinking to give you quality of life every minute of every day.

DAY 1

- AM: On waking, think:
  - 'How am I going to make today a good day?
  - How shall I think?
  - How shall I feel?'

- Use the Inner Modelling Technique.

- Lunchtime: Take a 10–20 minute walk outside. Observe your thoughts and feelings. Take 10 minutes to skim through the book and remind yourself what you learnt. This will help to put the information into your long-term memory.

- PM: Take a five-minute meditation or quiet time when you arrive home. Allow this to refresh you for the evening.

DAY 2

- AM: As you get out of bed, stretch and do five minutes' gentle stretching exercise.

- Lunchtime: Spend 20 minutes rearranging your office to make it an energizing environment. Observe your thoughts and feelings.

- PM: As you journey home, allow the pressure of the day to float away.

DAY 3

- AM: Eat food that energizes you. Taste the goodness of the nutrients you are taking in.

- Lunchtime: Review some of the decisions you have made in this book. Observe your thoughts and feelings.

- PM: Go home by a different route.

DAY 4

- AM: Focus your behaviour at work today on the aspects of yourself that you chose to be remembered by in the '85th birthday' exercise (see Exercise 2.8, page 28).

- Lunchtime: Observe your thoughts. Are they constructive and supporting you in what you are trying to achieve?

- PM: Do 20 minutes' exercise.

DAY 5

- AM: Plan the day ahead to enable you to perform at your peak.

- Lunchtime: How are you doing? Observe your progress. Support yourself with your radio exercise: tune in to Positive FM or Music FM (see Exercise 3.5, page 42).

- PM: Look back over the day. What did you learn about yourself?

DAY 6

- AM: Use mapping as an overview of how you are spending your time.

- Lunchtime: Monitor your 'pressure pot'. How are you managing your stress? Use the Three Changes Process – Changing your Thinking, Changing your Physiology, Changing your Circumstances (see page 60).

- PM: Get home in time to enjoy the evening.

DAY 7

- AM: Review this book. Take ten minutes to skim through your action steps and learning. This puts information into your long-term memory.

- Lunchtime: Listen to some music in your lunch hour.

- PM: Walk some of the way home and go via a park or garden if possible. Tune in to your thoughts.

DAY 8

- AM: Go to work with positive expectations of the day.

- Lunchtime: Are you causing any of your work colleagues stress today? Think about your own energy and behaviour and how it might impact on others.

- PM: As you go home, tune in to as many sounds as you can. Count them as you notice each one and let work thoughts float from your mind.

DAY 9

- AM: Use the Stepping Out and New Shoes Thinking models (see page 132) to consider other people's perspectives today at meetings.

- Lunchtime: Recall your Success Review (see Exercise 7.5, page 89). How can you use it as a springboard for success today?

- PM: Think back over the day. Were you assertive?

DAY 10

- AM: If you have a meeting today, use mapping as a tool (1) to get individual thoughts and (2) to combine thinking onto a flipchart or whiteboard.

- Lunchtime: Talk to someone you do not usually talk to.

- PM: Give yourself a treat – go to the gym, or have a massage, or sit and read a book.

DAY 11

- AM: Start the morning with diaphragm breathing.

- Lunchtime: Think how you could use facilitation in the meetings you have this afternoon.

- PM: Are you living your life by your values?

DAY 12

- AM: Decide to combine mapping with facilitation and run your meeting in half the time it normally takes.

- Lunchtime: Take five minutes to visualize your success so far and take those mental images into your successful future.

- PM: Notice any physical symptoms of stress. Are you tense around the neck and shoulders? Gradually loosen and relax your body.

DAY 13

- AM: Get ready for work in slow motion today. Believe you have plenty of time to talk to your family, or to read the paper.

- Lunchtime: Use the Three Changes Process to improve a problem (see page 60).

- PM: Are you projecting the role model you would like to those around you?

DAY 14

- AM: Focus on the Herrmann Thinking Preferences (see Exercise 11.2, page 144). See if you can identify the preferences of (a) colleagues or (b) clients.

- Lunchtime: Eat something you don't normally eat. Make it a healthy option.

- PM: How is your 'mental filter' (see page 33)? Can you feel your energy change as you change the quality of your thinking?

DAY 15

- AM: Take some coloured pens into work and use them to create maps.
- Lunchtime: Walk up the stairs for two or three floors.
- PM: What did you learn today?

DAY 16

- AM: Focus on the positive aspects of your life. What do you have that you appreciate? Count as many items/people as possible.

- Lunchtime: Observe the working relationship of yourself and your colleagues. Is it adult-to-adult? What could you do to change unconstructive behaviour?

- PM: Ring someone on your network and talk about your experiences.

DAY 17

- AM. Remember the Uplift Oscars (see Exercise 7.6, page 92) and run a movie of a successful day. See if it makes a difference to how you perform and how others communicate with you.

- Lunchtime: Are you living your movie?

- PM: Did your focus on your successful day make any difference?

DAY 18

- AM. Are you allowing real or imagined barriers to block your progress? How can you break through them?

- Lunchtime: Emotional check-up. How are you feeling? Are you managing your emotions?

- PM: Read a book to develop a multi-intelligence.

DAY 19

- AM: Look at yourself in the mirror and lengthen your spine. Decide to walk tall today.

- Lunchtime: Listen to some music during your lunch hour.

- PM: Appreciate your unique qualities. How could the qualities you regard as weaknesses be converted into strengths?

DAY 20

- AM: If you had to create an advertisement to promote yourself, what words would you use? What colours?

- Lunchtime: Talk to someone in a different industry sector to broaden your knowledge.

- PM: How did other people perceive you today?

DAY 21

- AM: Plan your next difficult event on the PEP planner (see Exercise 9.7, page 120).

- Lunchtime: Think about this question: 'How do I learn best?'

- PM: Who brought the best out in you today?

DAY 22

- AM: Focus on positive thinking today.

- Lunchtime: Take a two-minute meditation at your desk and allow it to refresh your mind so that you work more energetically and creatively.

- PM: Take a walk with a friend or family member and talk about what you are learning about yourself.

DAY 23

- AM: What is the one thing you can do today to improve your working relationships?

- Lunchtime: Rotate the chair or facilitator at meetings this afternoon.

- PM: Have a creative evening.

DAY 24

- AM: Use a MindManager map to help you analyse a problem.

- Lunchtime: Are you using both sides of your brain today?

- PM: How many roles did you play today?

DAY 25

- AM: Think about the Five-Step Thinking System. Are your values affecting your thinking? Is your thinking affecting your emotion? Is your emotion affecting your behaviour? Is your behaviour affecting your actions?

- Lunchtime: Do an exercise using the Inner Modelling Technique.

- PM: What was the percentage of negative thoughts to positive thoughts today?

DAY 26

- AM: Think yourself healthy today. Feel it in every pore of your skin.

- Lunchtime: Are you communicating with the global network today? Think about the people you are e-mailing or talking to. How many miles away are they? What cultures do they come from?

- PM: What can you learn about different ways of living when you think about people from diverse cultures?

DAY 27

- AM: Make some choices to manage your stress today.

- Lunchtime: Observe the different ways men and women work and communicate. How can you create synergy?

- PM: Go home on time and spend time doing leisure activities.

DAY 28

- AM: How can you bring creativity into your work and your meetings today?

- Lunchtime: Consider the office environment. Is it supporting what you are trying to do?

- PM: Did your language support your goals today?

DAY 29

- AM: Notice when you are being unreasonable and when you are being inspirational today. What makes the difference? Can you choose to be inspirational by changing your thinking?

- Lunchtime: Focus on your mission. How many steps have you taken towards it?

- PM: What was your behaviour like today? Did you bring positive energy into your work environment?

DAY 30

- AM: Review what you have learnt through this book and through your exercises. Remind yourself of the learning review system. One month is a good time to review information to put it into your long-term memory.

- Lunchtime: Take a deep breath in, look around you and find everything you look at pleasurable. Then go and look at yourself in the mirror and feel joy at who you see. Radiate your unique energy and contribution to those around you.

- PM: Give yourself a treat. Good luck.

Appendix 2

The Quicksilver Group

The Quicksilver Group is on the leading edge of individual and organizational development. To find out more about how The Quicksilver Group can help you achieve high-performance business results, please call or e-mail any of our offices.

Hong Kong

Quicksilver Limited
23/F Kinwick Centre
32 Hollywood Road
Central
Hong Kong
Tel: (852) 2827 7235
Fax: (852) 2827 4227
E-mail: chris@qsilvertlc.com

London

Positiveworks
60 Albert Court
Prince Consort Road
London SW7 2BH
UK
Tel: (44 020) 7823 8771
Fax: (44 020) 7584 0455
E-mail: posworks@netcomuk.co.uk

Miami

Quicksilver Miami
900 NE 195th Street, #606
Miami
Florida 33179
USA
Tel: (1 305) 655 2675
Fax: (1 305) 770 0926
E-mail: brainsell@aol.com

New York

Dottino Consulting Group
14 Lafayette Road
Larchmont
NY 10538
USA
Tel: (1 201) 666 5804
Fax: (1 201) 666 2728
E-mail: adottino@aol.com

Singapore

Buzan Centre Singapore Pte Ltd
95 Duchess Road
Singapore 269019
Tel: (65) 447 1866
Fax: (65) 466 2547
E-mail: dilip@pacific.net.sg

Stockholm

Quicksilver Sweden AB
Kyrksundsvägen 14
S-133 37 Saltsjöbaden
Stockholm
Sweden
Tel: (46 8) 748 9801
Fax: (46 8) 748 9495
E-mail: bo@qsilvertlc.com

Sydney

Quicksilver Sydney
PO Box 1051
North Sydney
NSW 2059
Australia
Tel: (61 2) 9954 0133
Fax: (61 2) 9954 0537
E-mail: tony@qsilvertlc.com

Zurich

Seifert Lagerkvist & Partners AG
Mainaustrasse 15
CH-8034
Zurich
Switzerland
Tel: (41 1) 381 7200
Fax: (41 1) 381 7202
E-mail: bo@qsilvertlc.com

Web site

www.qsilvertlc.com

Other useful Web sites

Herrmann International:
   www.thebusinessofthinking.com
Mindjet: www.mindmanager.com

Appendix 3

Further Reading

Amen, Daniel G, *Change Your Brain, Change Your Life*, Times Books, New York, 1998

Argyle, Michael, *The Psychology of Interpersonal Behaviour*, Penguin, 1983

Barrett, Susan L, *It's All in Your Head*, Free Spirit Publishing, Minneapolis

Bennis, Warren and Biederman, Patricia Ward, *Organizing Genius*, Nicholas Brealey Publishing, 1997

Berne, Eric, *Games People Play*, Penguin, 1964

What Do You Say After You Say Hello?, Corgi, 1990

Bettelheim, Bruno, *The Informed Heart*, Penguin, 1960

Buzan, Tony, *Make the Most of your Mind*, Pan, 1988

Buzan, Tony, Dottino, Tony and Israel, Richard, *The BrainSmart Leader*, Gower, Aldershot, 1999

Buzan, Tony and Israel, Richard, *Brain Sell*, Gower, 1995

Supersellf, Gower, 1997

Sales Genius, Gower, Aldershot, 1999

Buzan, Tony and Keene, Raymond, *Buzan's Book of Genius*, Stanley Paul, 1994

Cameron, Julia, *The Artist's Way*, Pan, 1995

Coleman, Vernon, *Overcoming Stress*, Sheldon Press, 1992

Cooper, Cary L, Cooper, Rachel D and Eaker, Lynn, *Living with Stress*, Penguin, 1988

Cooper, Robert, *Executive EQ*, Orion Business Books, 1997

Covey, Stephen R, *The Seven Habits of Highly Effective People*, Simon & Schuster, 1989

De Bono, Edward, *Six Thinking Hats*, Penguin, 1990

Dickson, Anne, *A Woman in Your Own Right*, Quartet Books, 1982

Drury, Nevill, *The Elements of Human Potential*, Element Books, 1989

Dryden, Windy, *Peak Performance*, Mercury, 1993

Dryden, Windy and Gordon, Jack, *What is Rational-Emotive Therapy?*, Gale Centre Publications, 1990

Edvinsson, Leif and Malone, Michael S, *Intellectual Capital*, Piatkus, 1997

Edwards, Betty, *Drawing on the Right Side of the Brain*, Souvenir Press, 1989

Ellis, A, *The Practice of Rational-Emotive Therapy*, Monterey, CA, 1979

Fast, Julius, *Body Language*, Pan Books, 1971

Gardner, Howard, *Creating Minds*, Basic Books, 1993

Gawain, Shakti, *Creative Visualization*, New World Library, 1978

Goleman, Daniel, *Emotional Intelligence*, Bloomsbury, 1996

Greenfield, Susan, *The Human Mind Explained*, Cassell, 1996

Gunaratana, Venerable Henepola, *Mindfulness in Plain English*, Wisdom Publications, Boston, 1994

Handy, Charles, *The Age of Unreason*, Arrow, 1990

The Hungry Spirit, Hutchinson, 1997

Hanh, Thich Nhat, *Present Moment, Wonderful Moment*, Parallax Press, Berkeley, CA, 1990

Herrmann, Ned, *The Whole Brain Business Book*, McGraw-Hill, 1996

Higbee, Kenneth L, *Your Memory*, Marlowe, New York, 1996

Holden, Robert, *Laughter, the Best Medicine*, Thorsons, 1993

Israel, Richard and Crane, Julianne, *The Vision*, Gower, Aldershot, 1996

James, Jennifer, *Thinking in the Future Tense*, Touchstone Books, New York, 1997

Jeffers, Susan, *Feel the Fear and Do it Anyway*, Arrow, 1991

Kotulak, Ronald, *Inside the Brain*, Andrews McMeel Publishing, Kansas City, 1997

Maguire, Jack, *Care and Feeding of the Brain*, Doubleday, New York, 1990

Moir, Anne and Jessel, David, *Brainsex*, Mandarin, 1992

Moir, Anne and Moir, Bill, *Why Men Don't Iron*, HarperCollins, 1998

Mukerjea, Dilip, *Superbrain*, Oxford University Press, Singapore, 1996

Brainfinity, Oxford University Press, Singapore, 1997

Braindancing, Brainware Press, 1998

O'Brien, Dominic, *How to Develop a Perfect Memory*, Pavilion, 1993

O'Connor, Joseph and Seymour, John, *Introducing Neuro-Linguistic Programming*, Mandala, 1990

Ornstein, Robert, *The Evolution of Consciousness*, Touchstone, 1991
Palmer, Stephen and Dryden, Windy, *Counselling for Stress Problems*, Sage, 1995
Palmer, Stephen and Strickland, Lynda, *Stress Management: A Quick Guide*, Folens, Dunstable, 1996
Parker, Steve, *Brain Surgery for Beginners*, Millbrook Press, Brookfield, CT, 1993
Peters, Tom and Austin, Nancy, *A Passion for Excellence*, Fontana, 1985
Pinker, Steven, *How the Mind Works*, WW Norton, New York, 1997
Richardson, Robert J and Thayer, S Katharine, *The Charisma Factor*, Prentice Hall, 1993
Ridley, Matt, *The Red Queen*, Penguin, 1993
Rose, Colin, *Accelerated Learning*, Dell, 1987
Russell, Peter, *The Brain Book*, Routledge & Kegan Paul, 1979
Siler, Todd, *Think Like a Genius*, Bantam, New York, 1997
Smith, Manuel J, *When I Say No I Feel Guilty*, Bantam Books, 1989
Smith, Rolf, *The 7 Levels of Change*, Summit Publishing Group, Arlington, TX, 1997
Stine, Jean Marie, *Double Your Brain Power*, Prentice Hall, New Jersey, 1997
Storr, Anthony, *Music and the Mind*, HarperCollins, 1993
Swarth, Judith, *Nutrition for Stress*, Foulsham, 1992
Sylwester, Robert, *A Celebration of Neurons*, Association for Supervision and Curriculum Development, Alexandria, VA, 1995
Tannen, Deborah, *Talking from 9 to 5*, Avon Books, 1994
Winter, Arthur and Winter, Ruth, *Build Your Brain Power*, St Martin's, NY, 1986
Wise, Anna, *The High Performance Mind*, Jeremy P Tarcher, New York, 1997
Witt, Scott, *How To Be Twice as Smart*, Parker Publishing, West Nyack, NY, 1983
Yates, Frances, *The Art of Memory*, Pimlico, 1966